# The World That Was the World of the Blackman

# The World That Was the World of the Blackman

*(And What Happened to It)*

An alternative account of
"In the Beginning" and accounts of ancient history

Hadja Aisha Cassana Maddox Nablisi

Copyright © 2020 by Robert Louis Maddox Jr.

ISBN-978-1-6485-8445-9

All rights reserved. No part of this book may be reproduced or transmitted in any form or by any means, electronic or mechanical, including photocopying, recording, or by any information storage and retrieval system, without permission in writing from the copyright owner.

The views expressed in this work are solely those of the author and do not necessarily reflect the views of the publisher, and the publisher hereby disclaims any responsibility for them.

Matchstick Literary
1-888-306-8885
orders@matchliterary.com

This, which I endeavor to document, must first be clearly understood to be from the perspective of an American Negro woman. One who differs only in having enjoyed the privilege of residing and working in Africa and the Near East, with extended privileges of travel in South Asia. There, I took advantage of invitations extended by friends and colleagues to visit with them in their countries and homes, where I encountered people with diverse ideas and knowledge, not widely exposed to my people of the Western world.

There are common traits that course through all humankind but reach divergent points, which classify us into various identifications we call race. Race is a word that is not translatable in ancient languages of the Middle East; however, it may have been native to the Aryans, who invaded the lands of black people of Hindustan. The Aryans were an endogamous people, who created laws for these black people—rules that became regulations with such punishments for transgression that they took on the profundity, becoming sacred and became the basis for a religion which established a caste system, which, I charge, became the roots of racism.

A system which I charge, no matter where these people in time progressed or traveled, no matter to what degree they managed to racially integrate with white people of the North World to remove themselves from the physical dark past of their ancestors, became one of their prime focus. They adopted or assumed the attitude of the Aryans centuries after the Aryans were racially absorbed into Hindustani society.

Herewith, I share with you, the reader, some ideas that appear to have some bearing on the subject of ancient black man and his world, which appears to have some bearing on his past, from people within the proximity of my travels, substantiated by earlier writings, which I have identified at the end of this volume—ideas that go far beyond that which we have been presented with as "white truths."

It should have earlier been apparent to all thinking men that the diversity of man must have, at some point, diverted due to some impetus, if indeed man ascended from a clot of life in the ocean as is accounted in recognized divine revelations and sacred books in recognized holy books.

I found an account in the Indonesian islands among a lesser racially mixed group. In Indonesia, racial intermixing has been practiced among black people yet there with Chinese immigrants.

Although the tale is intermixed with superstition and misunderstanding as to how natural phenomena operate, I found the idea perfectly plausible in light of developing knowledge and recent scientific information.

Granted that it is a generally accepted scientific idea that at one time the plates of earth were one; it appears that at some ancient time, planet Earth was hit by another massive heavenly body, perhaps even another planet. This is said to have struck the face of earth with such force that earth shattered into islands and continents.

But man, in his stage of development at that time, was not sequestered or limited to the east of Africa and the narrow straits of the Fertile Crescent but broadly spread out throughout the regions of South Asia, where the climate supported life.

He was similar in appearance and color, of Aboriginal characteristics, much the same as he appears racially unmixed, as he naturally appears there today.

This wandering object in space is said to have first struck in the region of today's Great Rift Valley in Kenya, circling north and east through today's Fertile Crescent into the region of the Himalayas, strewing in its wake a mass of dust, which I define as radiation. In time, surviving Aboriginal women, impregnated by men of her own kind, exposed to declining degrees of this radiation began to bring forth issue of a new type, exhibiting new characteristics of varying hair texture, skin color, and bone structure.

No plant or animal would have survived the direct impact of such magnitude. But in time, some issue much changed, survived. These I believe formed the beginning of those who in time became original white people.

Some may have migrated in small or large numbers to the more comfortable climates of the northern world. Perhaps some of their darker family members eyed them, in time becoming absorbed into their community. It is absurd to think that different types of ancient men, i.e., Cro-Magnons or Neanderthals, were lost or merely disappeared. Ancient men and their characteristics were merely absorbed and enveloped into the stream of humanity. Through integration with their brothers, they all shared sometimes positive, useful genetic traits.

I believe a more profound number of these new fair-skinned people appeared in Asia, wherein lies the greater number of humankind today. My hypothesis is based upon the research and works of the late Dr. Joseph P. Campbell. In this society with its penchant for establishing that which we are all to accept as truth, I charge that Dr. Campbell's world was forced to be written up as mythology.

His work of *Oriental Mythology* documents a tale attributed to some region of ancient India, events that I believe are of prime importance as to the origins of the white race, which is associated with an eventual tale of Adam and Eve, given in the Western-revered Bible, predating that era.

It appears that in the ancient days of early India, in superstitious days of much ignorance, there were children conceived and born, exhibiting much differing characteristics. Dr. Campbell does not identify these children as "white," but he does express their appearance as much different from that of the general population. Their difference was said to have held miraculous powers. The normal population is said to have been forbidden to mate with them, but these unfortunate children were said to have been permitted to mate and propagate among themselves, perhaps in order to assure a steady and ongoing supply of themselves.

About the age of fifteen or sixteen, a number of people among them were drugged and marched nude about the planted fields. Then they were stripped of their flesh and life. Their body parts were then planted among the seeds in the belief that such practice insured success of the crops.

Given the ability of man's inhumanity to man, I believe this tale as having more than a grain of truth. It also suggests that somehow, at some time, a large number of these unfortunates escaped northward. I suggest that the tale of Adam and Eve is a tale of two of such escaped beings. Not all of these people were necessarily subjected to horrible endings but escaped to the North World, finding there freedom and sanctuary in the cooler, more pleasant climes of the North World.

Reason tells us that these two beings were not singularly the only type of human species. The two conceived and delivered two offspring: Cain and Abel. Cain slayed Abel in time and then took a wife from a land east of Eden. Obviously, there were other people. Adam and Eve were not the beginning of a human race but were perhaps some type of a single people of whom other types were not considered equally human even at the time of the compilation of the Bible.

This intercepting heavenly body is said to have first struck in the region of today's Great Rift Valley in the east of Africa, cleaving out the terrain, circling north and eastward through the Fertile Crescent, east to the region of the Himalayas, strewing in its wake a mass of dust, I define as radiation. Aboriginal woman, impregnated by men of her own kind, eventually surviving exposure to decomposing degrees of this radiation began to bring forth surviving issue of a new type: without skin color, pale eyed, exhibiting new attributes of varying hair color and textures.

No plant or animal would have survived the direct impact of such magnitude. But in time, it is believed that some issue much changed, survived. These are said to have been the beginning of those who became original white people.

They may in time migrated in small and large numbers, to the more comfortable climates of the North World. Perhaps some members of their tribe or family of the darker number accompanied them, in time becoming absorbed into their early communities. It is absurd to believe the different types of ancient men, Cro-Magnons or Neanderthals, were lost or disappeared. Ancient men and their characteristics were merely enveloped into the stream of progressing humanity by integration, sharing with their brothers and sisters sometimes positive, useful genetic traits.

I believe the more profound number of these new fair-skinned people appeared in Asia, in Hindustan. It is there I base a hypothesis, supported by research and work of the late Dr. Joseph P. Campbell, whom I met with personally at his office in the School of International Affairs, Columbia University. Earlier I had read his work, which had been meticulously researched in India, Asia, and Europe; his findings forced to be written up as *Oriental Mythology*. Such in the past was the practice of dealing with the accounts of colored men's recollections of their past. Just write it up and assigned as mythology. Such practices are racism. Racism being a negative connotation or application applied to the experiences and accounts of the darkest of mankind.

Within Dr. Campbell's work on India, he documents a tale attributed to some region of India, events which I believe to be of prime importance to the white race and which precedes that which have been given in the Bible, associated to the myth of Adam and Eve.

His work does not specifically identify these youth as "white," but does denote that they were in some way profoundly different in appearance from the normal population, which we all know of as of a very intensely dark hue of skin color as found only there and in the southeast of Africa. In fact, these two areas give us the darkest shades of people of the black race. Yet Hindi denotes himself often as "white." What indeed is he trying to tell us?

Dr. Campbell tells us that these profoundly different children, I believe to be "white," were held by these superstitious people, in those days of ignorance, believed to possess mysterious powers by the difference in their appearance, enabling them to influence success of their planted crops. Mysterious rituals were performed with them, held by chiefs of these villages in which they resided. The normal population of these villages were forbidden to propagate with these unfortunate young people but they were permitted to mate among themselves. About the age of fifteen or sixteen, a number of people among them were drugged and marched nude around the fields at planting time and then set upon by the population who stripped them of their flesh and life. Their body parts were then planted among the seeds in the belief that such a practice would guarantee greater success of the expected crops.

Given the prevalence of man's ability to be inhumane to his fellow man, I believe this tale as having more than a grain of truth. It also suggests that somehow, at some time, large number of these unfortunates escaped northward. I further suggest that the tale of Adam and Eve denotes two of such beings who managed to escape. Not all of these people necessarily subjected to such horrible endings.

I reason that the tale of Adam and Eve denotes two of such beings who escaped. Not all of such persons doomed to ritualistic deaths, but eventually finding freedom and sanctuary in the cooler, more pleasant climes in the North World. I believe the allegorical site of the Garden of Eden to have perhaps been in the fertile valley of Bihar Province, Hindustan. It is clear that even the authors of the tale knew they could not have been the origins of human beings. As the story progresses, the two conceived and delivered two offspring: Cain and Abel. Cain slew Abel and then took a wife from a land, East of Eden. Obviously to any "thinking" people, there were other humans. The alleged "enlightened" European accepts his genesis originated in the east of Africa. I believe, however, that not all originated from a single area. But I do acknowledge that beyond skin color and texture and varied color of the hair follicles, man is uniquely and uniformly of a same kind.

History has been written over ten thousand years. We now find the white man in the cool climates of the North World; the darker and black man, native in the more warmer and hot world to the South, better enabled to reside there by the factor of melanin contained within his dark skin pigment, which protects him from the nuclear rays of the sun.

The written history of the European tribes begins with the writings of the Romans. Among these historians was General Agricola, conqueror of Britain, a world renowned historian. He recorded that his army encountered black people in Scotland, so fierce and previously unknown to the Romans. They were unable to conquer them. Who is to say, that even as far north as this region, black people did not journey there? Perhaps these dark skinned people accompanied kinsmen greatly changed or doing trade among those who had settled so distantly.

Unquestionably, man multiplied in the past as he has in the present. Periodically, his numbers have been reduced regionally by natural catastrophes, diseases, and death from predator's animal and by other human treachery of warfare and other calamities, which periodically have visited earth.

Today, 80 percent of the human population is nonwhite, 20 percent prime and secondary white. As we approach the new millennium, we all live in a new and enriching global environment where modern technology permits the on-site displaying of man, as he is, within his own countries. Yet I warn the viewer, what you are permitted to view is subject to censure, contrived by the racist policies which the cameramen are directed to focus. The visual appearance of the Aboriginal black man has often been subjected to restrictions, when the agenda is to project the appearance of others.

Indonesia is just one of the places in the South World where the media has chosen to present the countenance of either the Chinese or Chinese racially mixed Indonesian as the Indonesian. The appearance of the indigenous Indonesian is consistently similar to that of Aboriginal people from Guinea and New Zealand in East Asia, the Aboriginal people of Australia, and throughout the islands of South Asia westward, including the Adman Islands, the subcontinent of India where the people indigenously black are differentiated from their neighbors by bone structure and the follicles or texture of their hair, which is more akin to that of the Chinese people, their eastern neighbor.

The African appearance resurfaces again westward in the island of Mozambique and becomes again consistent from Arabia Felix to the east of Africa, including the interior of Arabic in Hofuf. The scorching heat of the desert makes life impossible to those of fair skin complexion. Only the most desperate and transient, even of a brown complexion with his entire body totally covered, could bear the brunt of the searing heat of the midday sun; much less become an inhabitant, permanently residing there with the modern convenience of air-conditioning. Racial integration has become a preoccupation of the American people, due to the overbearing instance of racial segregation during and after slavery in the United States. It did not, however, initiate here within this country and had been a practiced preoccupation among the human family for thousands of years. Perhaps it began at the inception of the occurrence of human differentiation among mankind in his state of development during that epoch of time.

There appears to have been two outstanding people of the past, the Romans and the Mongols, who have most influenced mankind in the Western world. Their people migrated, venturing forth unto areas of the world where man had migrated and dwelled in peace and seclusion wherein scattered, sparse civilizations were established.

In seclusion, wherein islands of peace permitted, established the beginnings of civilizations; some men maintained knowledge previously held by their earlier ancestors upon which they built, while others far removed geographically lost valuable information of what their group might have earlier known. Mankind has been outcast on the road of migration due to a number of reasons. In ancient times, as now much of this movement has been caused by invasions, famine, and ever-threatening war from neighboring tribes or even insurrections within the group. Famine created friction between the haves and have-nots. When men moved about the earth, they built their dwellings out of materials they found in new locations. They ate of what they found and had to relearn that which was safe by trial and error. They did not necessarily have time to transport tools and material for scripting, and the knowledge of writing became lost. Men, whose ancestors knew how to strip bark from available trees and plants, weave fabric, make looms and paper from papyrus upon which to script, were killed, grew old, and died especially upon long migrations. Ancient men were superstitious and kept knowledge secret, available to only certain initiates. When such knowledge was held by those who even might not have been among their numbers, expired before reaching passive destinations where they might pass on such worthy knowledge in new settings to the young who survived migrations, valuable knowledge was lost. In losing valuable information, man went naked; they might regress to having to reside in inclement weather without shelter and covering once known skills of the cultivation of seeds, of agriculture may be lost. Regression may result in physical genocide.

The Mongol people may have been driven out of their native region in Siberia, east of Russia, by a number of calamities which beset an unsettled—settling earth and humankind. Siberia, to the east of Northeastern Russia, sits at the top of the Rim of Fire, subject to devastating earthquakes and volcanic eruptions, which impact all countries on the Pacific Rim.

We hear of the Mongols in 3000 BC, in northern China, where in small groups, they repeatedly breeched the borders of the newly unified kingdom of China, under Emperor Shih Huang. The emperor had only recently unified the northern Chinese tribes under his kingdom's sovereignty. These raiding Mongol marauders threatened to disrupt this unity. Shih Huang ordered the initiating of the building of a wall to thwart their incursions. The wall was later added onto by succeeding dynasties, becoming known as the Great Wall of China. The Mongols were a cunning and clever people who first domesticated the horse, which was native to their region. They became the most skilled of horsemen. They are said to have been viewed almost as one with the horse by those upon whom they rode in on so swiftly, as to have appeared from nowhere. They were skilled archers and for centuries possessed superior weaponry, which they used with deadly precision. They apparently did not seek territory upon which to settle. They took mainly produce and livestock, and such as they encountered and may have needed, dispensing a quick death to those who unfortunately encountered or opposed them. They struck the north of China swiftly and left in the same fashion, taking no slaves or prisoners.

The period 3000 BC, over five thousand years ago depending upon whose calendar you employ, seems a period in time when mankind in many lands had long settled states, wherein they had established fine-tuned civilizations. These were mainly city-states, where areas of peace and tranquility, achieved mainly in isolated regions, were surrounded by seas of barbarity. Such a place was the ancient kingdom of Elam in the region of the Tigris and Euphrates rivers. As it was so close to northern Hindustan as to be documented by her historians, so must have Hindustan or India, as some of us yet refer to her, also been a great kingdom at the time, before the coming of the Aryans.

The longevity of such nations depended on the ability of their people to maintain formidable armies, create indomitable weapons always superior to those with whom they came into contact, whether challenged or as the challenger.

The Aryans, who swept down upon the land and people of Hindustan, appear not to have been resisted. But my information regarding this intrusion by whites upon these colored people stems from the white Western viewpoint, while the scant information allowed regarding the Hindi side emanates from sages and poets who more extols the alleged valor and style of the invaders. Indian poets tend to so glorify such invaders as the Aryans as well as Alexander the Great's armed invasion; one without the group would wonder whether the sacred texts which arose out of their interaction caused them, not intellectual subjugation but in fact, such awe of their skin color as a mark of desire to emanate but to hold their white invaders in worship. They appear not to have held any sense of respect of being of their naturalness; seemingly to only desire to associate themselves as being one with their aggressor who in observance destroyed their prior progress, which surely they had achieved as others had in their region, prior to the invasion.

The earlier invading Aryans seem to have been a contingency of priests, poets, philosophers, and keepers of the Aryans' sacred cattle. The larger number of their group, the Kshatriya or warrior class, were busy engaging in the conquest of Mesopotamia and Elam, the latter which fell only after a long period of time.

The first group established firm rules of endogamy. They are said to have prized their fair skin and long nasal appendage, disdaining the darker than mahogany skin of the Aboriginal Hindi, termed the Dravidians, with their wide flat nose.

The invaders are said to have been mainly interested in India's rich land for the pasturing and development of their cattle and took what land they wished for cattle development and growth of their herds.

There was to be no intermarriage among the Dravidians whose characteristics they disdained, but as nature would have it, soon after, there appeared within the Dravidian communities offspring obviously of a mixed racial type; the result of Aryan men and women of the conquered group. Proud Aryan women would not have been able to bring forth children by Dravidian men. The penalty was death. Such children of Dravidian women were not recognized as legitimate Aryans. They were not subject to Aryan privileges of inheritance or recognition. Early on, the populace of the conquered people was organized into castes regarding work duties. The primary caste system was not by status but by skin color. Under the system, a place was made for their obvious illegitimate offspring, who during the earlier days, before the arrival of the dominant warrior class, had already developed into large numbers, assisting and serving the priest who carried out the sacred rituals, libations, and led the sacred hymns.

Eventually, the second group of Aryans joined the earlier in Hindustan. These were the more dominant of the Aryans: the Kshatriya or warrior class. They lived to fight and die in battle. They held in contempt those who they described as prattling priests.

Upon their arrival, work occupations of the conquered people and caste, according to color, were more rigidly defined. Laws pouring forth with such severe punishments impacted so heavily upon the Dravidian, that in their written form, they assumed the sacred status of religion.

No code of laws, excepting Varna, applying to skin color or complexion, applied to all Hindustan. In the ordinary affairs of life, the place of law was that of Dharmashastras, metrical textbooks, which arose after the Kshatriya joined the earlier group, bringing with them the knowledge of written script from Mesopotamia. These metrical texts documented caste regulations and duties, composed by Brahman priest from a strictly Brahman point of view.

The oldest of these were the *Codes of Manu*, written by a Manava Brahman, intended as a handbook or guide to proper behavior for his tribe, the Manava. It gradually became a guide or code of conduct for the entire expanse of Hindustan.

Manu represented himself as the son of God, and said he had received his laws from Brahma himself.

In his codes, Manu warns the king never to tax a Brahman, even when all other sources of revenue fail, for a Brahman when provoked to anger, can instantly destroy the king and his army by reciting curses and mystical texts. The *Codes of Manu* were marked by superstition and an untiring inculcation of the virtues, growing rights and powers, which the growing Brahman caste people were creating for themselves. This effect was to enormously strengthen the hold of the caste system upon Hindu society. Gradually during extended peaceful times, war giving way to peace; religion, first an aide to agriculture in the face of incalculable elements, required expert intermediaries between man and God. The numbers of Kshatriya or warriors declined and gave way to other more peaceful pursuits. The once proud Aryans in time became racially absorbed among the Hindustani people. The class and growing power of the Brahman remained.

The importance of the Brahman and their knowledge of the Vedas marked them as the natural interceders to the gods, and the Brahman increased their numbers. The Brahman had been and were the teachers of the young. They were the oral transmitters of the race's history, literature, and laws. Long after the Aryans were racially absorbed, they were able to recreate the past and form the future in their own image, molding each generation unto greater reverence for the priests or Brahman, building for their own caste a prestige that would give them a supreme place in Hindustani society, which would last for over two thousand years. The position of the Brahman would outlast the rule of foreign conquerors, sultans, and kings. These exalted rulers mainly left India's caste system in place, overseen by the Brahman.

Understanding proper behavior was of extreme importance. Under Hindu kings, laws were extremely confusing; there was a mixture of royal commands, village traditions, and caste rules. Law under these conquerors was merely often the will or whim of the sultans and kings. Judgment was given by the head of the family or head of a village, headmen of the caste, court or guilds, governor of a province, minister of the king, or the king himself. Litigation was brief; judgment swift. Torture was used under earlier dynasties. Death was the penalty for damage to royal property or housebreaking. Punishment was cruel and included tearing out of eyes, pouring molten lead into the throat, crushing the bones of the hands and feet with a mallet, branding with fire, driving nails into the hands, feet or bosom, cutting the sinews, impaling men, sawing them, roasting men alive, trampling to death by elephants, or feeding them to wild or starving dogs. For a thousand years, these and other punishments were encoded into an understanding of law.

A fee was paid to these ministering priests as the most important element in any sacrifice to the gods. The highest summit of piety was the size given for sacerdotal wealth. For a fee, a Brahman might render a barren woman fertile. Oracles were manipulated for financial ends; men were engaged to feign madness and confess.

Their fate was punishment for parsimony to the priests. In every illness and lawsuit, for every bad omen and unpleasant dream, or when entering into a new enterprise, the advice of a Brahman was consulted and the advisor regarded worthy of his hire.

The Brahman's power was based upon a monopoly of knowledge. They were the custodians and remakers of a tradition. The exclusive experts versed in the inspired and infallible Vedas.

If a Shudra listened to the readings of the holy scriptures, his ears were to be filled with molten lead; if he recited the Vedas, his tongue was to be split. If he committed it to memory, he was to be cut in two. Such were the threats, seldom necessary to enforce, by which priests guarded their wisdom.

Brahmanism became an exclusive cult, carefully hedged around and against all vulgar participation. According to Manu, the most exalted among all the Brahman, a Brahman was, by divine right, the head of all living creatures. He did not share in all these privileges and power of the order until after many years of preparation.

He was acknowledged as twice born and regenerated by solemn investiture with the triple cord (a ritual carried out by other Brahman). From that moment on, he became inviolate. Manu had declared that all that exists in this universe is the Brahman's property.

A Brahman has to be maintained by public and private gifts—not as charity but as sacred obligation. Hospitality to a Brahman was one of the highest religious duties. A Brahman not hospitably received could walk away with all the accumulated merits of the householders' good deeds. Even if a Brahman committed every crime, he was not to be killed. He who tried to strike a Brahman would suffer in hell for a thousand years. If a Shudra debauched the wife of a Brahman, the Shudra's property was to be confiscated and his genitals cut off. A Shudra who killed a Shudra might atone for his crime by giving ten cows to the Brahmans; if he killed a Vaishya, he must give the Brahman a hundred cows; if he killed a Kshatriya, he must give the Brahman a thousand cows; if he killed a Brahman, he must die. Only the murder of a Brahman was real murder.

Under this ruling aristocracy were the Vaishyas: merchants and freemen. The Shudras, or working class, who comprised the mass of the native population and finally the Pariah—unconverted Chandalas or outcasts, war captives, men reduced to slavery as a punishment. Originally a small group, they grew to forty million and became known as "untouchables."

During this journey of life, the Brahman inculcated into the mass of the people reverence of the earlier Aryan's white skin color, which their own mulatto complexion now emulated. Many of these would, like the Aryan in time, become further absorbed into the masses of their darker brethren, creating a distinct brown race with moderate nasal features. Later and subsequent intaking of foreign white wives would bring in a number of fair-skinned people whose fair skin color was prized by these people, who so valued developing fair-skinned progeny through whom they believed they would reincarnate.

Granted that there are now Hindustani people, reputable scholars deny that the subcontinent was ever invaded by any "Aryan" people. These scholars' reasoning that there is an absence of any Hindustani reference to an Aryan race, I find it reasonable to assume there was a social incursion of a large contingency of fair-skinned persons, who at some earlier age came into the Indus valley and in time were absorbed by the indigenous larger dark population.

But let us take a view at the after-effect of such dictates. The masses of the people had no way by which to lighten their complexion, which in fact would have made no change in their work status. Under such a system, due to any subsequent lightening of complexion, they could not but help to have suffered low self-esteem. No man can help his looks, to which he was born. The problem became more pronounced in India (Hindustan) during the British colonial period, when India became the world's largest producer of films. Repeatedly written into her musical film scripts, Indian film princesses in scripts given to them by insensitive producers, generally mulatto themselves, verbally extolled to their lovers and boyfriends, thereby to their public, reminding the boyfriend, how beautiful and fair skinned they are. There is generally always the verbal attention drawn to the fair-skinned complexion of the female star. Not only is a dowry from a bride as large as possible, but also, these men are yet encouraged to marry up a bride always to be two shades lighter in complexion to bleach out the natural color of his progeny.

This mind-set and practice was transported everywhere the Hindustani people traversed regardless to what religious persuasion he might adapt to, especially in the Western world. It was by such philosophy, he transported the roots of racism.

Racism is not a phenomenon that came unto the Western world out of nowhere. The ancient Romans brought to the West an appreciation of the source of white women of the Germanic tribes, from whom they might recreate their own countenance unto that which they most appreciated and desired for themselves.

The small number of descendants of purer white people in the world who reside in the far northern regions of Finland, Iceland, and northernmost Sweden appear to be people who are more relaxed of their being. These people are in the native countries inhabited since their native ancestors inhabited this region of the world and are constantly being threatened by unexpected, uninvited arrivals of large number of secondary whites.

The genesis of these secondary whites in Europe has in the past initiated in north India, stemming from interracial marriage with oriental-white women. Mating not only coming from the orders of the Macedonian upstart, Alexander the great to his generals and soldiers in Persia, but also the practice of mating with oriental whites from white tribes from the upper rim of the mountainous regions which separate the Soviet Union from India, Georgia, Azerbaijan, Turkmenistan, Uzbekistan, Afghanistan. Turkey, when it was Constantinople was a state containing thousands of original white people before the coming of the Romans.

Then, re-conquered by Mongol armies, Bulgaria, Romania, many people of Herzegovina, Bosnia, Romania, Yugoslavia, Albania, Hungary, and Greece to the West have all contributed to the human gene pool having substantial numbers of secondary whites. The continuous arrival of such people into these areas even today create heated issues regarding territorial intrusion, possession, and overcrowded populations, resulting in continuous warfare. The tendency of these evolved, landless people was and yet is, to gravitate from the lands of their dark ancestors; to gravitate toward the lands of the fairer of whites, wherein they erroneously believe they would be welcome as if the space of land is infinite. Europe lying at the western end of Asia is a surprisingly small area of the world. Even if larger, its lands cannot support the continuous stream of humanity now pouring there out of Asia Minor, Pakistan, India, Africa, and the Far East.

The leaving ex-colonists obviously did not think through the possible consequences of their intrusion into Hindustan, Asia, and Africa. Even to me, it is amazing that so massive a number of former colonized people would freely choose to follow their colonial masters to their home lands, live and work among them, opting to apply taking citizenship in these countries.

In Hindustan, when the British arrived and established their presence as a governing power ruled from the far off British Isles; among both people, there was an understanding of historical relationships which had not met previously uninitiated eyes. Among the wealthiest and politically powerful British, there were those who knew of the ancestral relationship with Hindustan.

Many in India, especially the Raj class attributed the genesis of their ancestry more to and with these white men rather than association with the indigenous darker Hindustani people, native to this land. These new British invaders were in part most acceptable to Hindustani society even reminiscent of those who had preceded them thousands of years ago. Like the Aryans, they brought additional legal order, reorganized economic life, and expanded and introduced international trade. Initially, they left the Hindi ruling class of the Raj in place. The status of the Brahman were left intact and even greatly benefited from the new legal ideas of inheriting property, an idea they quickly adapted, extracting even greater gratuities of land bequeathed from the dying faithful.

The masses of the Hindi poor, burdened over the centuries from tilling the soil, weighed down by the obligations of correct behavior within and among the castes, were earlier burdened to seek education or better improve their life. The wiser among them, no longer willing to settle for the imposed way of life put upon the people of their land, escaped South and East, dwelling among other people with whom they had to contend, to Indonesia, Malaysia, Java, Burma, Singapore, and southwest, to the burning deserts of southern Persia (Iran), Mesopotamia (Iraq), and Arabia, which hardly supported life, but where men often traversed upon the trade routes to Misr (Egypt), Libya, and northward to Greece. They further intermixed with all of the people of these lands. Their children later moving north and westward into Europe. This integration much enhanced by the coming of the Romans into the seven hills.

I was initially stunned when informed by Hindustani colleagues at the university in Tripoli that the Romans came from India. Returning to the United States by way of London, I stopped and stayed awhile long enough to ascertain that indeed this was true. It was common knowledge to the academic scholars and to learned English people in fact.

To any scholar, who have bothered to read India and the Vedas, the basis of her culture, the consequences of such a fact calls for a new ground of reflection on everything, especially the development of the church and its dictates. Rome, not Israel, was the land which determined the origins of the faith.

The Bible, compiled and written by the 7 and the 70, was not accepted by the church and forbidden to be read by their faithful until a much later date. The people, who prefer to be called the Jews are well aware that all adherents of Christianity are psychology bound to acknowledging them as associated with the Christ. And they, in great error, associate religious reverence for Christ with political allegiance to their interests.

A Westerner, regardless of his race, cannot become a free man until he has first researched the dominant force behind Roman culture; the Vedas. More to the point, any would-be knowledgeable Westerner or scholar must research the Vedas, especially those scriptures pertaining to "varna" which relate to skin color. It may well be that the oriental whites who conquered Mesopotamia and subsequently Hindustan might have been one of the same people.

These were the people under Sargon II, Sennacherib, and Esarhaddon. They were the conquerors of the most Western early civilized black city-states. Elam, which was a city-state which lay north and east of the river Tigris, was a highly civilized city-state contemporary in its development with that of ancient Egypt. Dr. Nilakantra Sastri, the renowned Hindustani historian of the University of Mysore, India, identifies the people of Elam, as having been "Negroid." A term we know well in the United States as having thick, tight-curly, dark hair, black skin as it was in those days in all of the regions adjacent between India and Africa, another trait, full lips, attributed to all the people between and of Asia and Africa.

Dr. Nilakantasastra's description is confirmed by the large amount of sculpture and depictions on the pottery obtained from Elam's site, which has been carted off to Great Britain's museums even as has her inscription writings of her past.

It is to Elam that we must next turn our attention.

During the time of Elam, the Persian Gulf stretched some hundred miles north into the interior of the land. Elam was situated north of the Persian Gulf, east of the Tigris River, occupying the rich fertile plains and the mountains to her north, now known as Khuzestan province. The Persian Gulf extended up on the Elam side to Ahwaz. There in this region of the world today known as part of Iran, she established one of the earliest civilizations. It owed its prosperity to its hot, alluvial plains and its vigor to the mountains, which made up most of the country. Its capital city was known as Susa, its biblical name Shushan. Mention of it can be found in the biblical books of Nehemiah and Esther. (Neh. 1.1, Esther 1.2) has also been referred to as Susiana and was known to the Greeks as Elymais.

To our interests, at her earliest time, she was peopled by a Negroid people as they have been attested to by the mass of sculpture and inscribed artifacts collected from the site.

In historic times, her people spoke neither Indo-Aryan, Sumerian nor a Semitic language. Their language survives in a written copious cuneiform. She has left extensive amount of literature (mainly kept in

British library archives), and her language was spoken as late as 1000 BC. Elam never moved to build an empire and was an independent state, subjected to constant warfare in defense of her borders. This once secluded highly civilized state developed during times of tranquil peace became constantly challenged by derivative Mongol forces militarily successful in surrounding city-states which had been usurped. The armies of the Mongols, reinforced by the procreation of soldiers with conquered native women, continuously sought to break through the borders of Elam. She withstood onslaughts from Sargon II, Sennacherib, and Esarharddon by these Mongol derivative people often referred to as the Assyrians. Elam was a flourishing city-state in 3000 BC. Her golden age, however, came after 1200 BC under the rule of Shutruk-Nahhunte, the greatest Elamite general.

Shilhak-Inshushinak was the builder of the Elamite civilization. Under Shushinak, the language was revived and put to literary use; an architectural and sculptural renaissance took place. Constantly under invasion by Sumer (3000 BC), Kish (c. 2850 BC), King Sargon (2800 BC), Elam overthrew the dynasty of Ur (c. 2300 BC) and began a short period of aggression, marked by the sacking of Erech (2280 BC), carrying away an idol only restored to Erech when Susa was sacked many centuries later. Assurbanipal finally conquered her about 645 BC, and Elam disappeared as a state but her language was spoken as late as 1000 BC. Her artifacts and literature, however, are stored in the British Museum.

The British have carted away, under their colonialism techniques more than merely the Elgin sculptures of ancient Greece. Only the Greeks object today. Egypt is not herein widely treated as she has been well treated by European and other writers, except to make comment of her people as associated later in this document with the Romans. Fortress Egypt was also breached by the Hyksos, another branch of the Mongol invaders; there, Esarhaddon sacked Memphia in 681 BC. Egypt's armies crumbled under the armies of the Assyrians. She lost and then regained some of her territories, ruling only over some provinces.

Later, Alexander, the Macedonian, invaded Egypt as he had the known world. Upon his death, he willed Egypt to his good friend and comrade, Soter Ptolemy I, ancestor of the renowned Cleopatra, who was not exactly a black woman, as all too many think, unless we measure bloodlines of racially mixed people with people of African descent with infinite precision. For purposes herein, Cleopatra was a Greek, of the twelfth dynasty of the family of Ptolemy family rulers in Egypt.

The massive numbers of fair-skinned people we find in Egypt today are descendants of conquered white European slaves of the Romans, now interracially mixed with the black indigenous Nubian people of Egypt. Egypt was used by the Romans as a human depository of white European slaves. They have since undergone much absorption into the indigenous population.

This treatise concentrates on little explored readings and subjects of historic interest to the Western diasporas. Designed to set the record straight, it is hoped to lead to fostering further research, by younger would-be scholars who manage to get to regions the world important to the black experience, as well as research materials locally available in different languages. However, there is no substitute for on-site research The past of our people, brought to the Western mainland of the United States to the slave markets of the Carolinas and Virginia, has been particularly and deliberately concealed. One might wonder, why would those among the white man (I now recognize it is a serious wrong to lump them all into one category), who engaged in so much chicanery, lies, and deceit, would so destroy links to the people's past.

Why was this course of action, done to the particular people brought to the mainland of North America, carried out? Why was it so necessary to erase memory of their past? What had the ancestors of these people done to have so enraged the policy makers who instigated the great Atlantic slave trade? They made bulging profits from the slave labor, taking these people out of Africa. Under no circumstances could these profiteers been our ancestors, comrades, or friends nor are they our trusted friends today.

Thus I continue to work to unsheathe this research, which I have undertaken from a number of references, sources, and writings in other languages. Some of the answers lie in sources of other languages such as Arabic, a black language utilized at the University of Timbuktu, yet the widest used on the African continent today.

Paid agents of "the devil," utilized by the devil's control of educational institutions, are often placed there where it regard those who descend from slavery, to have those who know little of their true past, instruct those who know even less.

They have been empowered with "empty degrees" for this purpose. They oftentimes distribute misleading and misinformation, designed to delay our broad-based intellectual development. Remember, these are the same people who denied us, during slavery in this country, the right to learn, read, and write under pain of death. This is a country wherein its leaders dare to refer to other states as "evil empires."

The evils of this country, earlier outstripped the evils of some of Great Britain's large number of Africans, have been brought to the United States, trained and placed in universities and even set up to head African and African American studies departments, as if they held some type of expertise of their history in Africa.

Even the greatest African University in Africa today, the University of Ibadan, has received input regarding the ancient history of African people and regions from the Yiddish speakers. The truth is, the African, in at least West Africa does not know his ancient history. Most Africans, who teach in American universities, have received their training in either Britain or here in America, generally from white sources.

In the great city of Kano, where I discovered the vast store of documents which had been carried overland from the University of Timbuktu, those in whose care it resides, Muslim black men held the idea that the history is best kept unknown. Truly the African mind, as well as his value system, is not the American mind.

The African immigrants, like all the other third world (including inner-Europe,), come to this New Babylon with either a vague or no idea of this citadel to which they have come. They come to this bastion of capitalism of which they know little, perhaps after hearing of some vague entity known as democracy.

Democracy has been extremely loosely defined in their native countries. I have encountered many of these lesser literate people "out there." A taxicab driver in Arabia, noticing I spoke English, who wished to practice his knowledge of the language, told me, I couldn't possibly be an American. The Americans were all six foot, blond white giants. When I displayed to him my passport, he became very elated. He then told me that he was going to immediately apply for a visa for himself and his family and come to these shores, which he has most probably achieved by now, these twenty years since.

Arabs are a people of the South World, who dwell on that barren hot desert. Without the advantage of modern air-conditioning, it is hostile to life. The term *Arabs* belongs only to those indigenously living in that desert, not to those of whom you are advised as such by white Jewish owned and controlled newspapers and their press. Take care, not to be caught up in the mainly politically emotional agenda.

The regions on the rim of the Persian Gulf supporting life as in D Dhahran, Hofuf, Al Khobar, barely comfortable. The peripheral states of Bahrain, Dubai, Abu Dhabi, Oman have cooling ocean borders. To the south, the Yemenadjacent to Somalia, Ethiopia, and Eritrea in East Africa are open to the Indian Ocean support sedentary life.

These oriental Jews promote the idea in the West, of these Greeks as Arabs and Semitic, to validate their own appearance similarly as Semitic. But the truth behind this idea truly raises more questions than answers which I shall later both raise and address. As I have earlier stated, Palestinians, Lebanese, and Syrians are Greeks by blood and only Semitic or Arab by culture, when living in their own environments.

The Arab are, as most men in these regions of the world are dark-skinned, indigenous people. They have in the past socially crossed paths with various white people and exchanged wives. Offspring from such issue are naturally generally fairer than the father and darker than the mother. The Arabs, certainly the African Arabs, are yet basically a racial mixture of India and Africa, retaining a dark, swarthy complexion and sometimes a more coarse texture of loose, curly hair.

Many Europeans that think of themselves as solely white are actually secondary whites. These people are products of racial integration earlier in Inner Europe, Asia and Asia Minor in Pakistan, North India, and areas of the Middle East; long before their ancestors moved westward to Europe and the Americas. It has only been recent, since 1965, that these people were permitted to migrate to the United States, a land even less tolerant of racially mixed, nonwhite people. A nation which worked long and hard with racial segregation in order to prevent this country from becoming a nation of racially mixed white people. Little did they reckon on the political power, will, and leadership of the oriental Jews who have come en masse out of Russia and Europe and so affected policy in America.

Man out there in the "old world," has historically in past time, moved in a cyclical fashion, coming into contact with one another, engaging in social intercourse, intermixing his genes. The tendency of fair-skinned issue, as well as that of their darker brothers, has then been to intermix with those like himself coming to a plateau, moving on to ever intermix more with those who are even more fair skinned, until as a group they settled and established themselves in uninhabited spaces.

Distance themselves from the group, moving ever further on northwestward, their offspring yet migrate to enjoin with the white North World. The Aryans moving down into Hindustan and other parts of the South World were merely returning to the land of their ancestors much in the fashion of sea life returning to the place of their birth in order to lay their eggs or spawn.

My only question of Ancient man is, who were the Mongols? It is said that they originated in Siberia. A well kept secret from even the European is just how victorious they were in battle, even from their beginnings and of their impact first upon White Russia. The feats and intelligence of some of their derivative people are so remarkable, at such an early time in man's intellectual development, so commonly far beyond most people that one might suspect they migrated from a superior distant other world. Paramount among these intellectually superior people are that segment of Mongol people are those we call the Jews.

It is said the Mongols first swept westward out of Siberia into Russia in small bands initially, creating havoc and laying waste to village settlements in Russia. They took no prisoners, killed the men, and were probably the first Asiatic people to kill all males and rape all young females of child-bearing age. The male issues of such unions, holding no loyalty to their father land, were then trained to join with and ensure, growing raiding parties to aid in raiding other neighboring settlements.

By such practice, early Asiatic conquerors continuously enlarged their armies. In early Asia as now, boys were removed from maternal care before the age of ten. They swiftly swept down upon villages, as if appearing out of nowhere, terrorizing the people, most of whom had no knowledge of the horse which was native to Siberia, domesticated and rode upon by these men. They were such skilled horsemen and rode in so suddenly as if out of nowhere; victims thought man and horse were one entity. Altering the continence of survivors by racial integration with survivors, they created new types of people wherever they went, with differing physical attributes. Differing Asiatic whites developed in Russia, various oriental whites developed among the Chinese, Indo-Chinese, and other Far Eastern oriental people.

Although we think of their homeland as Mongolia, they also settled in Uzbekistan, Turkmenistan, Tajikistan, Turkey, Hungary, and Kazakhstan, the latter, a most important place. Here, the Grand Khaqan, ruler of the Khazar people in Kazakhstan, converted to the Hebrew people's religion in the year 978 BC during the reign of Solomon the Wise, ruler of the city-state of Jerusalem. Eventually, defining themselves as Jews, leading to a course of philosophy, by which ever steering themselves; not upon thrones, but the power behind Western thrones, they would come to lead the world.

Kazakhstan Province sits in the South Central region of the former Soviet Union. At one time it formed part of a greater region, stretching from the Caspian Sea into China, extending into southern Russia. A rich agricultural practice existed there in earlier times. She also is rich in oil, and her mountains are rich in lead, zinc, gold, copper, and an array of precious stones.

From the earliest times of recorded history, her people became among the most knowledgeable and skilled metal smiths and jewelers.

It is not clear to me how they managed to join into the entourage of people we know of as the ancient Romans. One might guess, however, that they were in ancient times a clever adroit people then, as they are today. Early on even in ancient times, they had commenced to trade over vast regions of their known world. Wherever they went, they seem to have developed a keen knack of observing and noting the habits of people, the useful skills and practices of a society. These practices they learned and spread this knowledge among their people.

Roman history has been sadly neglected in the United States for some malevolent reason. It is cloaked in mystery and mysticism. Rome beginnings attributed to the tale of its leaders, Romulus and Remus, twin sons of Rhea and Mars Silva, who were allegedly taken out into a forest and exposed, but were found and suckled by a she-wolf, thus surviving. Found by Faustulus, a shepherd, they were reared by him and his wife Larentia. For our purposes they marched into the Etruscan region of the seven hills we have come to know of as Rome about 753 BC. At the head of an Asian military contingency who either purposely undertook this route or having been cut off in some battle, engaged in some military excursion further east. In accordance with armies of the day, they were accompanied by a large number of camp followers equal in size to a village, a common practice in that day.

There would have been craftsmen, especially metallurgists or blacksmith repairmen, tent erectors who put up and took down portable shelters, slaves to do the heavy labor, cooks and food tasters, slaves to keep and clean various utensils, weavers and tailors to create and repair uniforms of the soldiers. Slaves to pasture and tend the horses, care for the fowl and cattle. Wives and children would accompany these armies to its rear.

And there were the Jews, skilled in the practice as counters and treasure keepers. The Jews were the Talliers of Roman wealth, skilled in the new technology of writing and reading. They were masters of this Mesopotamian art, which the soldiers, occupied in fine-tuning their skills in battle, had little time to pursue. As counters and keepers of the Roman's treasures, they were adept, valued, and rewarded for their services. Many Jews became extremely wealthy, were freemen and widely engaged in extensive trade over the vast regions of the empire. Some Jews were appointed governors of Roman provinces, and there was among them some who were unfortunately poor.

Clearly we can now see, there were two distinct differing groups: the Semitic Hebrew people, Semitic by blood and those who had earlier adopted to Judaism.

And I wonder, if this might explain the dichotomy of opinion in the account of Pontius Pilate, asking of the Jews, whether or not they revered Jesus, the Christ, as king of the Jews. The Khazar certainly abstaining, abhorring such an idea; the other Jews, the Hebrew, responding positive.

Pilate, the more familiar with the Khazar, the Khazar a Mongolian people, holding respectable, responsible positions as keepers of the treasurers of the nobility and the wealthy would have had the greater influence. The Hebrew/Semitic people became an obscure people. Remnants of their people migrating to Yemen, Ethiopia, and other areas mainly in East Africa, settling and surviving on this continent until modern day Israeli settlers have come to collect them to give validity to those to whom the covenant was given, among their kin there.

The vast majority of the Ethiopian, the Oromo, are also a Semitic people.

Rome was under attack, most of her history. The Germanic tribes attacked Rome to her north and west, the Dacian attacked her southern flank, and constant uprisings and rebellion threatened Rome from within. There was also the rise of the troublesome new sect called Christians, mainly servants and slaves who began to question the rules and standards and those who had declared themselves gods in Rome. From the beginning, the rulers of Rome had sent their dissident detractors of

Roman thought in exile to the far north of the British Islands. These now highly fair-skinned Romans sent there when the empire was stable were greatly joined there when Rome was rife with rumors of collapse of even her more remote parts of the empire.

The practice of such migrations stepped up as rumored collapse of nearer areas of the empire reached Rome. Family members were dispatched along with trusted servants with large stores of portable wealth of gold and jewels. These Romans did not resemble the Romans as their ancestors had been when they arrived in the seven hills. They now blended in well with the people of the North World.

In Britain, with their massive wealth brought there, their descendants as well as the descendants of Jews who scattered there and other areas of Europe, set the foundation of wealth which they built upon. Their descendants are among the wealthiest of Europe today. In southern Europe, the Jews progressed to become bankers and architects of governance. The Jews defined a way of life in Europe. Eventually, members of their group supported established monarchies. As man united and progressed, they created both the system of capitalism and communism which then set out to compete as one system with the other. Some have forgotten the latter system improved the lives of serfs, who were enslaved by despotic, insensitive monarchs.

Like the Romans, some have a penchant toward breeding themselves even whiter, but they also are clever sufficiently to breed with a wide number of groups investing in their progeny, training them to become leaders of lesser developing groups. The greater group seeks now to become leaders of lesser developing groups.

Let us return to the more important aspects of information regarding Rome, which have affected the destiny of our people: the rise of the church and the formation of acceptable doxology, theology, and the business of the church.

The instrument of the Bible and the rise of the institution of the church were entirely two totally separate, unrelated matters.

Before the coming of the Romans, western Europe was sparsely inhabited save for Germanic, Celtic, and other tribes, who lived a sparse existence. Its people were scantily clothed in skins, flaxen woven garments, filthy of body, and resided in scattered thatched huts. They were recently moved to the sedentary stage and practiced rudimentary domestic animal husbandry and the planting of simple agriculture. When the Romans were driven to engage in repeated battles and forcefully establish their sovereignty suzenity over the hapless scattered tribes, they cleaned up the people, instilling upon them the value systems which they held and had brought with them. The Romans united the disheveled people; improved housing, food preparation; organized them into villages, towns, small cities. They brought into these places clean water and encouraged them into improved personal health habits. The Romans in time, built advanced roads and aqueducts which transported water from sources far away. Marketplaces were developed and goods shared first by barter, later by coin and currency.

The Romans were strict and said to have been cruel masters when opposed. The empire was never without a constant threat of siege and the empire established afar eventually stretching to far for the armies required to keep in check.

Constantly Rome was threatened by intrigues at home, assault from without, continuous revolt within the provinces, and there were the Christians and the growth of their movement.

Continuously, thousands of Roman dissidents, now both wealthy and quite fair skinned, were sent to the British Isles where they were later joined by thousands threatened by marauding Germanic tribes, who sought their freedom from Roman rule.

The formerly enslaved and now poor freemen of Rome took refuge down in the catacombs which lined the lower space of Rome where Roman citizens buried their dead. Due to the heavy fighting and wanton destruction in the city above, poor innocent civilians were often caught up in the middle of increasing Germanic and other raids. These battles beset all of the townspeople; burning their dwellings and destroying their scant possessions. Thousands had become homeless. At the end of Rome's defeat, during a lull in battle, these disheveled, unwashed people with scant provisions began to emerge from the catacombs and construct scanty huts of earth and straw as had their ancestors in lands, far from the place where they had been brought or come. Some among them approached the rabbi, the known learned ones. Some of these had earlier held secular administrative positions of lesser affairs, concerning the poor and the slaves, well represented among these numbers. The hapless but inquiring European asked of the rabbi, the Jews also known as the people of the book, to give them a book by which they might know themselves.

Seven rabbis are said to have collaborated and have assembled for these Europeans an assortment of known Hebrew accounts of human creation, beginning with the fragmented tale of Adam and Eve, of which I have already expounded my theory; based upon my assessment of Prof. Joseph P. Campbell's work. I believe it to be substantial fact. His work was conducted on site, in India, without a doubt in my mind, the Western power structure, which will not tolerate differing opinions from which I term "white truth." Truths not necessarily devised by descendants of original white people, who are comfortable in their being of themselves, but by their insistent masters, those who have racially infiltrated in among them to whom they are now spiritually and thus intellectually bound.

European history formally begins with accounts documented by the Romans. The common European people do not know their history, of the tumultuous long suffering of their people's past. Their written history begins with the writing and collections of the Romans, who should be credited also with having built Europe for them. They carved out the nucleus of today's European great cities. They established for them a system of basic laws, upon which they have built. And as Rome fell as a state, the princes of Rome created a new form of political and social leadership. This organization was called The Holy Roman Catholic Church, wherein the princes of the land maintained and continued to employ the skills of their leadership abilities as princes of the church.

The church, in its infancy, was a political entity. Only after determining its structured offices, the roles and functions of its officials and their assignments did it long after undertake in numerous heated debates in synods and councils religious policy to be taught and unquestionably accepted by European people.

Even in the fifth century, the common European people yet lived in thatched huts in a wet climate of isolated people, eking out their existence on simple farms. Many of these survivors were people whose ancestors had known other lands. But had no means or knowledge how they might return. After the collapse of the empire, the land and people reverted back to a stage, sometimes below the condition the ancient Romans had encountered when they arrived in the region. But the knowledge of many of the survivors had been enriched by the knowledge of many skills that the empire had collected, diffused among many common workers and passed on to their children. I do not hasten to document this writing but am fully aware that others in the third world are coming out and learning of the interest in Westerners in learning of their homelands' places. I have met with Pakistani and Hindi colleagues, who have come out since world war II, to Europe, armed with their own regional histories of the past and of their ancestors' association with events in Europe, little known by the common European.

Many of those I term secondary whites emanate from the so-called Middle East and North Africa, where they are hardly white but of a racial mixture. They now en masse travel out to northern lands to find there; they are not received as white. In Benghazi, one of my Pakistani colleagues painfully exclaimed to me, "We built Europe for them, and now they don't want us there." Recently, on a Saturday morning Hindustani television program, *Namaste*, some Hindi scholars stated, "They now know, they don't merely descend from the Aryans." A matter, not entirely true perhaps. A natural assumption of the so-called distinctively fair skinned among them. I reserve any assessment of them racially, based upon observing them in London's east end.

In London, the English, the poor, who are unfortunately oftentimes ignorant, point out these mainly refined, gentle people in their native dress, exclaiming, "Look Roma, Roma."

The people of Hindustan, Pakistan as well as Bangladesh and Sri Lanka, whom I met while lecturing out in North Africa and the Middle

East, are among the most pleasant, well refined, and well mannered anywhere in the world, certainly among the most likeable in any society. Rather than misunderstand each other, it would be better if we were to attempt to research, learn, and uncover the dynamics behind the actions of various differing people.

It is insensitive of any British or Englishman to so criticize the people of India. The people of India, or Hindustan as they now preferred to be called, display values no different than that of Italians, who fancy and frequently have sought German, Swedish, and Irish brides.

In the West Indies, in Jamaica and Puerto Rico, both formerly Spanish colonial territories once with a large population of black African female slave populations, has produced thousands of evolving fair-skinned populations. While in Hawaii, scarcely few dark-skinned, pure, indigenous Hawaiian people remain. The Arab in Arabia and North Africa has widely engaged in interracial marriage with the European that in Libya; so many of their young men, let out to study in Europe, brought back home so many white females of shady character, that the government, incidentally a democratic government, having an elected Congress, elected to pass laws, forbidding their people to freely travel outward without express government permission.

Such actions has also occurred among other young men in other Arab countries, who have found desirable females in the Euro-American environment, married with them and had begun families in these host countries with little care, that the laws of paternity quite differ in the West.

Additionally, the perception of race is viewed and often seen mistakenly. I recall quite clearly, during a documentary, on the story of the history of Western oil exploration, near the end of the series, regarding the invasion and response to Iraq's invasion of Kuwait, the ex-Saudi Arabia Minister of Petroleum Sheik Yamani clearly stated, "We had not expected the United States to come to the aid of this African country." The indigenous people of Saudi Arabia, especially from the region of Hofuf, to which most of the tribes yet hold in the highest state of respect, are hardly less African as are the indigenous Kuwaiti. Such racist reflections, as stated and preserved on film by Sheik Yamani, come from those who have come out of Pakistan and from some in India, who yet harbor their opinion of being different from the tribes of the desert, who have raised them up and set them in lofty positions.

Thousands in Saudi Arabia are not Arab, nor native to the region. Many are no doubt nonbelievers, feigning religion in order to enjoy the rich life in the state. Such are merely Saudi on paper, and if the oil were to dry up today, or some other renewable energy source were discovered changing the course of fortune, they would fly out faster than those who in fear fled out of Hong Kong at the leaving of the British to various white countries of the North World. In the countries in the third world with large Pakistani, Indian, and oriental people, change moves on a very slow track.

Many errors of perception misunderstands the effects of change in attitudes in the West regarding race, religion, and who and how one is allowed to participate in politics and function in American big business considerations, resources importance, and economics, the latter a social entity. On the other hand, I observe among men is the only slightly brown skinned, believes in great error, that in the West, he is on a somewhat higher level than his only slightly darker brother because of only a slight difference of complexion. Nothing could be farther from the truth in the United States.

There is also in the Middle East and some South Asian regions a notion that a political and military alliance is formed when the white man in America allows his daughters to be carried off in marriage to the foreign land.

This thought is not valid in the West. Just as in the West, children are seen as being best off with their mothers, whereas in some Eastern countries, wives are understood, to bring forth children for the benefit and stewardship of the male parent, as if the female has contributed no genetic material to the effort other than to have borne it for nine months, delivering it into the world beyond her womb. There are other serious misconceptions which lie between people of the East and West.

Such people in being permitted to immigrate and reside in key Western countries will sometimes face a harsh reality of this place of which they have held only mythical illusions knowing little factual information of the United States before their arrival. Some will elect to return to their homelands.

I have encountered people from Pakistan, I met in Saudi Arabia who in great error informed me they believe the fair skin color of the white race marks him as being pure in the eyes of God! Equally at the other end of the spectrum, the black man is marked by disfavor with the entity God. All seem to attribute this to the illogical tale of Ham and Sherri. The alleged people are within the biblical world, the South World, where men are naturally of a dark color. In the Bible, the color of this black son, Ham, is racistly attributed to his having viewed his father's nakedness at a point in ancient times, when men in fact had little coverings and probably at sometime saw not only their father's nakedness but occasionally that of their mother's and sister's.

Such racist fragments of ignorance contained in the Bible did not initially appear as articles of faith embraced by the Roman Catholic Church, which in fact was the original Christian church and architect of its one true faith.

There is no question that men are as afraid of the unknown today, as ancient men of yesteryear. Men today as well as men in ancient times seem to need antecedents willing to act between man and God. Fear is the force which drives men to seek solace from a spirit world. Christianity for two thousand years gave solace to those who earnestly believed that a God, in whom they were of his image, had died hundreds of years ago for their wrongdoings. No matter what evils they did, they need not pay for it. Such understandings of the white man's concept of Christianity surely was of great comfort to those who pillaged the earth, taking as one chose of places and resources, already inhabited by people of color.

Then, during the renaissance, the popes, bishops, and other high officials of the church in Europe employed large numbers of skilled sculptors and artists to embellish the churches, entrancing the people and binding them psychologically to the faith with depictions of the holy family, especially the holy mother and child as Nordics.

The artists were innocent. Most were simple but talented men, who had never traveled outside of Europe. They painted as instructed by their patron, "The Church," whose officials we assume were knowledgeable. With careful instructions and expectations, they directed and monitored the artists' work, directing deceptive characterizations of the Semitic holy family in the image of the fairest of white European people.

Such depictions affirmed to the European white people they were indeed created in the image of their God, accompanied by ideas of this God having been sacrificed by crucifixion for the forgiveness of their all-time sins, later bolstered ideas such as "manifest destiny," free handed taking the lands and resources of the third world, as well as so blatantly embarking on the business of the great Atlantic slave trade.

In America, this effort was accompanied by centuries of tumultuous inhumane depravity; while teaching the people of these lands, their actions were sanctioned by a one true faith. Is it any wonder that a Polish, non-Roman pope would apologize to the world for wrongdoings by the church.

The inculcation of Christianity was done at a heavy price also to masses of whites. Men did not so easily give up their ancient time-honored concepts of the Godhead. Before this new religion was accepted throughout Europe, hundreds were tortured and had their possessions seized and confiscated by the church during the period of transformation.

Papal Bull 21 was issued sanctioning the churches' permission of the beginning of the great Atlantic slave trade. In this economic endeavor, there was an economic alliance between this vestige of ancient Romans, who now acted as princes of the church and the descendants of the Mongols, both even now heavily altered by the effects of racial integration. The latter engaging in social intercourse with the, lower class, but fairest of Europe's people.

The Spanish monarch had regional power but not the wealth to initiate either the Atlantic explorations or the business acumen to institute the business of African slavery though had motivation, given their recent victories over the Moors.

The business and trade of African slavery was a scheme of the Sephardic Jews, a matter covered in the volume, *The Secret Relationship between Blacks and Jews*, an essential must read compilation which should be read by all, who would seek the truth about the financial motivation behind the trade. The business of North America is business. In the Western world, wherever there was business to be done and profit to be made, the Jews have always been collectively in the forefront, acquiring wealth and somewhere near, behind the visible figureheads of power.

As a people, we must never forget atrocities done to our people, of which the greater crimes here in the West were the continuous destruction of the family, By this, the eradication of our history, our languages, the erasing of ancestral cultures, such destruction of our past, we are yet, in the twenty-first century in a very generalized way attempting to research and amend.

Some of our past languishes behind the veil of different European languages, known by some, but alien to most of us, who exist in the English-speaking world.

Such matters may lie in the Spanish and Arabic languages.

Of those who in the early sixties denounced Arabic as a white language, some were innocent, others may have been agents of those who wish to maintain intellectual control over blacks. We cannot as a people get caught up in the rhetoric and agenda of the Jews and their problems with the Syrians, Palestinians, and Lebanese who are in fact Greek by blood and merely Arab by culture; although by the system of taking wives in marriage, these dark men of Arabia may in fact have fathered these offspring with white women of the North World. It is even said by white Arabs whom I have known that when these men took many wives, they invariably made slaves and servants of their dark sons, sons who the more resembled them and raised their fair-skinned sons to more lofty positions. Under any circumstances, Arabic was and is the language in which the history of Africa lies, and this included the documents stored within the Great Mosque of Kano, northern Nigeria.

In the sixth century, the Syrians broke through the borders of North Africa. They did not bring their women with them; they took wives among the indigenous black women of North African tribes. They remained there for two hundred years before number of them moved on.

During this time period, long after the Romans, there was extensive social communication between these dark-skinned people and the Germanic people who ruled in Spain.

There, there were intratribal disputes among the Visigoth tribe in what would become southern Andalusia. Roderick, a Visigoth strong man and reputed villain among the Visigoth, had usurped the throne of former king Witizia and also ravaged the young beautiful daughter of one of the noblemen, Count Julian of Ceuta.

At the time, in the year AD 711, North Africa was ruled from Damascus. Musa Ibn Nusayr was the appointed governor of North Africa. He had received his prominent position by having led the troops who had driven out the Byzantines from all territories in and west of the Carthage trading settlement.

His troops had gradually pushed their conquests to the Atlantic Ocean, uniting the Nomadic tribes along the way. By 711, the people inhabiting North Africa were a racial mixture of indigenous African and Syrian; these people in time became known as Berber or North African Arabs.

The Vandals, Germanic tribe had retaken and ruled in Spain since the fall of the Romans. Leadership after the recent death of their king was challenged by Roderick, inciting his many enemies, among them the powerful Oppipan, bishop of southern Spain and brother of the late king Witizia.

Count Julian appealed to Musa Ibn Nusayr to come to Spain, confront, and defeat Roderick and restore the son of Witizia to the throne.

Count Julian supplied the number of ships by which troops, horses, and the required military supplies were transported across the thirteen-mile stretch separating North Africa and Spain. Musa Ibn Nusayr dispatched his most trusted and able lieutenant Tariq ibn Ziyad, a Berber to carry out the mission. Tariq ibn Ziyad insisted that the mission be carried out by his seven thousand Berber troops. His forces were aided by Count Julian's men. When Tariq ibn Ziyad's Berbers encountered Roderick's men, they quickly dispatched them, abetted by dissension within Roderick's troops and rebellion among the populace. Witizia as well as Roderick had severely persecuted the Jews of Spain, who rose up in dissent during the invasion. Roderick was usurped and escaped during the invasion and was never again seen. Victorious Tariq moved his troops unexpectedly north to Toledo without orders to do so by Musa Ibn Nusayr. Musa Ibn Nusayr, upon hearing of Tariq's move, allegedly sent a message to Tariq to halt his invasion and return to North Africa.

It is not historically clear whether or nor Tariq ever received the message. Tariq continued to dispatch detachments to Elvia, Archidona, Cordoba, Malaga, and Ecija where his forces encountered the greater resistance. Musa, back in North Africa and said to be jealous at the success of is lieutenant, rushed into Spain with ten thousand troops, all Arabian and Syrian. He had Tariq put into chains for disobeying orders. Witizia had expected to be restored to the throne; but now Musa, supremely in charge of ten thousand troops who had accompanied him and now seven thousand Berber troops previously brought by Tariq, continued the Moorish invasion; moving north to Saragossa, Aragon, and Leon. He then moved to the Asturias and Galicia in autumn of 713. There Musa was recalled to Damascus to face the same charges he had earlier made of Tariq. Musa left his son, Abd al-Aziz, in charge in Spain. He cleverly chose a retinue of four hundred Visigoth princes to accompany him to Damascus. The royal princely entourage clad in resplendent dress, wearing golden crowns and girdled in gold, were followed by thousands of European captives and slays, all carrying a large store of treasure and captured booty to be delivered to the caliph, Al-Walid, momentarily dying from a longstanding illness. The king's brother Sulaiman, chosen successor to the throne, sent a letter to Musa to delay his triumphal march into Damascus. His brother dying, Sulaiman wanted Musa's grand entrance into Damascus to coincide with his soon-to-be-celebrated ascension to the throne. Musa declined, news of the richness of his procession traveling before him.

Such a rich procession had not been seen since the fall of Rome when Roman legions had returned from their military campaigns of conquest loaded down with slaves and priceless loot, captives from distant lands previously unheard-of by most of the population These captured lands, like Spain, were then incorporated into their empires as provinces. Reports of the triumphant procession arrived in Damascus before them, news reaching the dying caliph, Al-Walid, so enthralled him; the news is said to have revived him temporarily, much to the anger of Sulaiman. Musa entered Damascus in February 715, and was received with great favor by Al-Walid, who expired two days later. Sulaiman promptly had Musa arrested, punished, and humiliated. Musa was made to stand, uncovered all day in the broiling sun, until he fell from exhaustion. He was removed from all authority, his personal possessions and property confiscated. His final humiliation was to come later when the head of his son, Abd al-Aziz would be presented to him at court.

After Musa Ibn Nusayr departed Andalusia, his son, Abd al-Aziz, took as his wife Egilona, widow of Roderick, forcibly raped by the victor, she bore him a son, now becoming known as Umm-Asim. Egilona was unforgiving of the defeat and plight which had befallen her, and she created brilliant schemes by which she extracted revenge.

Egilona, a Christian, persuaded her husband to take on Visigoth usage of wearing a crown. She had Abd al-Aziz to have the entrance to his royal chamber reconstructed. The entrance to the chamber was made so low, no one could enter without bending as in obeisance. She also insisted on having a door to her palace chapel, behind which lay the entrance to her bed chamber made so low, Abd-Af-Aziz had to bend on entering as if in an act of worship. And Egilona had rumors of all these behaviors exaggerated, embellished, and carried back to the caliph in Damascus, making the Muslim Emir, appear to have converted to Christianity.

Suleiman, promptly ordered Abd al-Aziz's execution and beheading. The year, 716, Abd al-Aziz's head was presented to his father at court. Musa later died, impoverished in an obscure village in Syria.

The now Syrian-Moorish invaders remained in Spain over eight hundred years. They subjugated and inhabited areas from the river Ebro to the Atlantic Ocean, from the base of the Pyrenees Mountains to Gibraltar. During the period of their reign in Spain, millions of African Berbers poured into Spain as settlers. They had formed the base of the forces who had fought there and complained that the Syrians appropriated for themselves, the most fertile areas of the regions, leaving for the Africans, the least undesirable scrub areas. Throughout the Moorish inhabiting of Spain, there was always periodic regional dissention. During the reign of Caliph Al-Nassyr, in Ak-Zahra, the caliph had surrounded himself with a bodyguard of "slays." numbering thirty-two hundred men, who headed an army of hundred thousand. The term "slays," was applied to slaves and prisoners captured by the Germanic tribes and others sold by the Germans to the Arabs. The term was later applied to all purchased foreigners; Franks, Lombards, Galatians purchased young and then Arabized. With the aid of these, now called Janissaries, or Mamluks, of Spain, the caliph kept treasuries in check and reduced the influence of the old Arab aristocracy to whom they held no loyalty.

By 1090, racial lines in urban communities were hard to distinguish. Arabs from Syria among the army of conquest and colonialists were comparatively few, limited mainly to those in command and in high office. From the beginning, Moorish women among them were in small numbers. Disease and fighting decimated the early conquerors and settlers. After the fourth generation, Arab bloodlines became quite diluted by intermarriage with native Spanish women. European concubines, slaves, and prisoners of war helped in the process of amalgamation, as in other lands.

By 1090-1147, the dark Muslims had become overwhelmingly of Spanish blood. The rough Berbers in Spain, raised on the deprivations of the desert, transported to the luxurious regions of Morocco and Andalusia soon succumbed to the vices of European civilization. They became inebriated and even effeminate. They entered Spain as settlers at a time when intellectual and sensual pleasures had long replaced a love of war and thirst for conquest. These formed the Murabot and Muwahhid dynasties of Spain. Their ruling seat was based in Africa, in Morocco.

From 1199-1492, the Nasrid sultans, who traced their ancestry to Al Medina, in Arabia, were the ruling sultans in Spain. The Nasrids, unable to cope with a danger of losing their Andalusian kingdom, increased their appeal for military aid to North Africa to no avail. Their Berber brothers, sovereigns in North Africa, were busy fighting among themselves.

While the Christian reconquest of Spain initially started in the eleventh century, it was to continue until after 1492; many of their kinsmen, prisoners of internecine warfare back on the continent were to be sold into the great Atlantic slave trade. Northern Germanic tribes had never accepted the sequestering of Spain. Border areas had to be defended from spasmodic attack throughout Muslim reign. The process of reclamation was greatly accelerated by the union of Castile and Leon in 1230; Toledo fell from the Moors in 1085, Cordoba in 1236, and Seville in 1248. In 1469, the marriage of Ferdinand of Aragon and Isabella of Castile united the two armies of these kingdoms. This marriage marked the end of Muslim power in Spain. By 1492, Ferdinand with an army of ten thousand entered Granada. An agreement was initially brokered with their Catholic majesties to leave the Muslims secure in their person under their laws and free to practice their religion. This was later rescinded by Ferdinand and Isabella. A campaign of forced conversion began in 1499. Arabic books were burned and the inquisition began.

In 1501, all Muslims were to recant Islam or leave Spain. Millions began to flee to adjacent islands and North Africa. Final expulsion was ordered in 1609. A half million were expelled: landing on North African shores, in fury, joining those who had entered earlier, levying vengeful raids upon their North African brothers. The battles enlarged into full-scale war, all the way down past Mali, committing their captives into the new slave trade which fed the Americas.

While accounts of Muslim conquests of Spain is generally known as well as the Germanic reconquest and expulsion of the Moorish descendants in English, lesser known, but of even greater significance to the African diaspora in the West is the internecine warfare of North

Africa. These battles also destroyed the Great University of Timbuktu, in Mali, so far southwest did the fighting penetrate. The University of Timbuktu was well known and highly respected. Scholars from all over the known world at the time came there to research, especially in the field of medicine, science, and astronomy. These scholars also joined in lecturing and teaching.

Its medical facilities devised and successfully performed the most delicate of neurological and eye surgery, unknown and practiced in Europe of that time. As news of battles further north progressed southward, this news was received by the University of Timbuktu's officials in Mali. It prodded them to prepare to safeguard as many documents and other written material as possible. They entrusted the safeguarding and transporting of these properties to the Tuareg traders, who in several caravans transported these library materials to the far, inland south, overland through the desert, depositing them in the city of Kano, in what is now known as northern Nigeria, where today, these materials lie rotting within the Great Mosque of Kano. There I discovered their existence safeguarded by Islamic forces, from destruction by malevolent interests, sequestered from the Christian whites some of which would not hesitate to destroy any documents of the historic black experience they might acquire.

Decay and time is causing these materials to decay. But some might be salvageable, the problem to be encountered by the northern Nigerian keepers of the mosque who might only be persuaded by money.

Because a man shares a resemblance to you, because he is of what one may perceive to be the same race as you, may be, but does not mean that he shares your same value system. He may not even hear that which you say, even when he understands the language in a general form.

These materials, I would imagine hold information, almost sacred proportions for the Western black scholar in the diaspora. I would grant that they would also hold great interest to a scholar of any racial persuasion. Naturally, all material therein, with the mosque from the university, is written in Arabic; the language of that time and place. Learning that fact, in northern Nigeria, Niger, and Mali, was the motivation which so fired my inspiration to pursue learning the Arabic language, until I acquired some facility with the language, which led to my applying for and receiving the greatest honor I could ever have received; being brought to the Royal Kingdom of Saudi Arabia on a complete scholarship to study advanced Arabic, Islam, which is my religion, which should be explained to the world, means righteous guidance. Righteous guidance being man's main, continuous, and oldest pursuit.

Righteous guidance being that which all men of good will continue to seek, to do the will of God, being man's main continuous and oldest pursuit.

It is essential that any would-be African American scholars of ancient black history, known of the existence of this material in Kano, just that further and existing research done in other languages be translated into English; English being utilized by so many people of the world, especially the greater number of our people in the diaspora. Spanish and Arabic are necessary vehicles in order to research and translate material for broader knowledge. They are essential to be studied for historical research. They hold vast stores of knowledge, especially regarding what happened to people taken from the Niger River area to the slave ports of Jamestown, Virginia, and Fayetteville, North Carolina.

It is said that Dahomey slave port was responsible for over 20 percent of the people exported. But the majority of these people were sent to Brazil and the Caribbean. The history of the trade is a well-documented business record, and those records are intact and can be found in the U.S. Library of Congress with other references intact to sources in European cities' libraries.

Most important, it is essential to acquire and read in English, Dr. Phillip K. Hitti's volume *History of the Arabs*, especially regarding the internecine warfare which broke out in North Africa as the expelled Moors returned home and turned violently against their brothers in North Africa, wars which stretched ever further south.

The people taken out of Africa and brought to North America were according to the records of the slave trade as documented in the U.S. Documents Illustrative of the Slave Trade, which can be purchased from a publishing company in New York mentioned in the credits page of this volume. Within its pages, it refers to those who were to be bought into mainland United States; "Bring us not those with wide nostrils and thick lips, they will frighten our women and children."

These people were most likely had not experienced a long period of time in Africa's Northwestern region. Such characteristics as ordered, and slavery was a business, denote people who had long been exposed to racial integration, similar to the traits of the Somali.

The Africans of more substantial proportions were taken from unfortunate people further South and West and transported to areas of Latin America and the West Indies plantations. There, white people thought of as less gentile, resided, most of them men. These were the stronger of the slave people. Some of their numbers were brought onto the mainland later to breed with the group there to improve their stamina.

All of these unfortunate people were victims of the same trade. I have personally been in the company of Africans who recount that indeed, some of their ancestors engaged in the Atlantic slave trade, which was the basis of their wealth. In Togo, the king is said to have even sold his mother-in-law, who was said to have been meddlesome in his affairs of state. Save for those in the north and eastern rims of the coast of Africa, the face of the American Negro, that is the adult American Negro of the 1900s, is not commonly found in the west of Africa, as is the lesser racially mixed West Indies of the same time period.

On the continent of Africa, the people most resembling the American Negro are the Somali and the Eritrea Oromo. This is not necessarily because they are of one and the same, but because each group has undergone similar racial integration with similar people.

I would concur with the thesis of the late Honorable Elijah Muhammad, who constantly referred to the black man in North America as being indeed an Asiatic black man.

This is easily concluded from observation when traveling in these regions and given the thousands of years of man, constantly moving about the earth.

I believe those people who settled farther south on the West African coast, as the people of Angola, were undoubtedly those there the longest and may represent a number of the original people of Egypt; Nubians who built the early Pyramids, who migrated earliest out of that great civilization.

The Angolans enjoyed an early stabilized monarchy and form of government and an extraordinary civilization in Angola as viewed and extolled by early Europeans who encountered them far beyond the others on the continent. Such structures would have required a long period of peace by which to form such a civilization.

All of the people on the west coast claim historic accounts of having migrated from the East. Obviously a great deal of coordination is required to unearth all of the facts between interested parties among the diaspora in the West, and African academicians on the broad subject of African history, in the proliferating universities on the continent. All too often, we in the America view the subject of racial integration as an interplay between the white European and people of African descent. This is not so. Most of the people of the Middle East and South Asia are racial mixtures.

South Asia is a melting pot of black, oriental, and Chinese people. The Hindi, both themselves widely migrating for various reasons as well as being transported by the British as middlemen, wherever the British went, became a third tripartite component of integration, intermixing in regions wherever they went.

Additionally, it is said, of the vast difference between the Chinese and the Japanese, the Japanese are of an Indonesian oriental racial mixture. Perhaps the most universally beautiful people in the world.

My personal interest in ancient black history ends with the beginning of the great Atlantic slave trade, in which there is much interest among us. Slavery is a subject which has been and which will undoubtedly be even more explored in the future.

There are a number of other incidents in the history of black men, which must also be researched. Now that the people of the world have undergone a vast surge toward progress under the new world order, men will come forward from all areas of the world and bring with them their accounts of their past. Visits and cultural exploration should be directly made with the black indigenous people of New Guinea, New Zealand's people and with those few, now nearly extinct in Australia.

Social interaction should be encouraged to document within their own words, their view of their ancient past and their assessment of their historic predicament as affected by interlopers with whom they came in contact.

At this time, in this volume, it is necessary to backtrack to post-Roman history and explore secularly the advent of the beginnings of the Holy Roman Catholic Church in order to somewhat trace the transmission of ideas, which took root in ancient Hindustan and were transported and transplanted into the culture of church doctrine.

The Roman Empire was established about 753 BC. Earlier, before the migrant intrusion of the region by Romulus and Remus and their entourage, the region was inhabited by Etruscans, Sabines, and Latins. We may assume that if these people were not pure white Europeans, as were the Germanic tribes at the time, they were most certainly a fair secondary white people who had gone across to Europe earlier in time. This is not to state that they had not been a people who had traversed to Europe along with their initial white brethren. General Agricola, Roman conqueror of Britain and a historian, referred in his writings to a fierce, dark race his army encountered in Scotland, whom they could not conquer.

Herein I refer to people who propagated and developed into large numbers of original white tribes. I refer as some originals: Vandals, Ostrogoths, Visigoths, Alemanni, Subei, Tirol, Franks, Cimbri, Burgundians, Celtic, Teutons, Helveti, Salian, and Ripuarian Franks and others found indigenously at the top of Northwestern World.

These people in the past have been under assault for their physical attributes for integration from orientalized people of inner Europe. Such was achieved mainly through their lower classes. Some of their people were transported eastward, managing to retain their genetic kind as the people in the former Soviet state of Georgia.

There is worth mentioning, the greatest crime of genocide carried out against one of an innocent black people, the people of Tasmania their plight without comparison ended by genocide, carried out by British Australians.

From 1688 through 1783, England enjoyed enormous growth at home, of her domestic and international development. The early eighteenth century saw a rise of inventions and of domestic machinery. Albeit these early machines were manufactured of wood, they were none the less proficient in relieving man from a portion of heavy labor. Landlords saw these inventions as no need to maintain compensated wage laborers at the time, who although employed, were barely compensated sufficiently to maintain life and support of their families.

Men deprived of work and wages by which they sustained life were oftentimes driven into towns, villages, and cities where they were unsuited for the type of work and commerce they found there.

The British Maritime absorbed men who met horrible conditions and low wages and for a period of time, work had been created from the trade of transporting rum, molasses, and slaves between Africa, Europe, the West Indies, and the Americas.

The British government flourished by the energy and skill of her commerce, expanding her educational institutions, creating niches of positions for enterprising excess sons of the nobility whom the crown employed in her service. But as often during a time of growth and plenty at the top stratification of a society, the gap between those at the top and those at the bottom grew insurmountable.

Mid-eighteenth century, women and children of the displaced poor, who had fled the changing agricultural regions, pouring into the slums of the towns with commerce, managed to gain employment in the factories. They toiled there sometimes in the most deplorable conditions from twelve to sixteen hours per day for subsistence wages which barely sustained life and shelter. In some places, the condition of their lot in life was so poor that dwellings were rented out in shifts, wherein one slept upon mattresses of the most filthy conditions during the hours of their tenancy. These dwellings were without even the most rudimentary sanitation facilities. Chamber pots were used in which to deposit their bodily waste. These were unceremoniously frequently dumped from upstairs windows containing of urine and fecal matter, upon any unfortunate passerby who might not be so fortunate as to escape their aim.

Entire neighborhoods reeked of the stench of human and animal waste. Diseases, i.e., cholera, tuberculosis, and venereal diseases were rampant. The numbers of those who died of such conditions were quickly replaced by newcomers to the slums, who sought any type of work from the cities' wage labor.

In the coal mining regions of England, European women and children were often harnessed like dogs to draw the coal carts down into and up from the depths of the mines with the heavy contents of coal. These workers some as young as four to six years of age spent as much as eighteen hours a day, squatted down in the coal dark darkness. The short life span of such laborers was of casual concern to the capitalists. There were plenty of these poor whites, all willing to replace any fallen domestics on shore or drowned at sea.

The era of free unbridled capitalism and the fortunes of the empire took a turn for the worst, near the end of the eighteenth century. There was a revolt in her thirteen North American colonies. There was war with the French and the beginning of much disgruntling of high taxes at home, regarding revenue upon which the state depended. Additionally, as usual, there was the problem of a seemingly ever-increasing poor: worrisome beggars, pickpockets, prostitutes, and other criminals the state wished to do without.

By 1817, the balloon burst. England was sunk deep in the mire of an economic depression with a criminal element at home, on the verge of revolt. Of this era, author Clive Turnbull states in his book, *Black War*, "At a period like this, when the honest and industrious scarce knew which way to direct their energies, the occasional but favorable accounts transmitted by antipodean citizens, opened a prospect to the British government, whereby they might get rid of some of their clamorous and redundant population." Great inducements to emigrants were offered. In order to overcome any scruples, passage in some cases wholly, in others, in part were given upon the embarkation of the emigrant. Rations were supplied for the first six months. Land, free of quitrent was granted not only to the father but promised to be conferred in fair proportions on each of his children. As part of the compensation for the land granted, the settler was to maintain a certain number of convicts. From the point of view of the British government, this system served a number of answers to its problems.

That the land for which they were destined, Australia and the Tasmanian Island, had already had naturally indigenous occupants was incidental to the British government. Their government did not with sincerity, care for the poor among their own people. The Aborigines of Australia and Tasmania or Van Diemen's Islands were not even remotely considered a matter of account. To the British government, a burdensome number of free surplus of her citizenry were thus gotten rid of. Her felons were efficiently disposed of without cost to the crown. A means had been found, in initiating penal colonies to Australia, whereby people might be induced to emigrate.

Now let us try to look at the situation from the view of those felons accused, most of whom were undoubtedly guilty but some of them innocent, as among all men imprisoned.

Among these were men, women, and sometimes very young children transported in chains, sent forth on a journey of three or more months. Transported in chains, they were to be permanently removed from England, from all whom or what they knew in their homeland. These so deported, were not merely felons. It was seen profitable to remove the excess population from the insane asylums, all fit persons from the almshouses, except the most aged and helpless.

The seafaring crew was not humanitarians and their behavior toward their charges was oftentimes brutal. They took sexual license with the women: free women and felons. All of these people encountered alien terrain upon their arrival. Penal colonies were not idyllic and welcoming. The Tasmanian people were also not happy and overjoyed at seeing the continuous arrival of ever more usurpers of their lands.

The European white settlers were met with an abundance of new problems upon arriving and attempting to settle into the structure of the new society. These unfortunates languished socially at the bottom of British society, wracked in poverty and living a dejected existence were nevertheless a part of a social structure wherein all, were vested in their unifying comfort that they being white, were born in the image of their God.

A God, who they had been taught, had died for any wrongdoings, that they might now or in future commit.

Exhausted from a long and uncomfortable journey, most of them weak, badly fed, they were seized and shocked with fear at the native Aborigine, whose very countenance reflected all that they understood, embodied evil. The Aborigine was tall and black. They often insisted on appearing before them stark naked. Even the women, who covered their shoulders with kangaroo skins, left their private parts, most covered in polite European society, bare to the colonist view. And these new colonists were not immigrants in the free sense. Australia and the settled adjacent colonies were loosely disciplined penal colonies where men and women, deemed guilty of the most nefarious crimes, were physically free. The free men and their families were subject to malfeasance from them, as they imagined would come from the blacks. The jailers and authorities who managed the diverse society were quickly outnumbered by ever arriving of English ships, bringing a continual rise in both criminal and free men population.

In time, settlers and free men came to fear more than the convicts, who came to overcome their fear of the bush and were called bushrangers. Settlers and free men were left to their own volition, clearing away the brush, planting crops which sometimes failed and caused settlers to compete with the Tasmanians for their ever-growing scarce food supply. In their quest to satiate the natural sexual lusts, they often killed Tasmanian men, to take their women. The feared bushrangers raided the European settlements which they converted. Settlers were brutalized and murdered. Women were ravaged and raped. When caught, crimes against the white populations were generally punished by hanging. But bushrangers, settlers, and freemen all hunted down and systematically murdered the Aborigine, even organizing sporting events for the occasion. In England, all problems encountered in the colonies were expected to be handled by the local colonial administrators, who were weighed down in the colonies trying to deal with the myriad of common daily problems which were insurmountable. Their main focus was the administering of a penal colony, encumbered by the mundane, troublesome task of dealing with grumbling free men and settlers. Little time was left to spend on the additional problems of Tasmanian Aboriginals as they had been advised by the crown back home. The greater administration was the abundance of communication reports, which flowed back to the English government and the massive directives on paper. Unfortunately, the administrators in the settlements had little manpower and force, by which to protect the Aborigine. The doom of these black people, so far from civilization, was preordained when the white man came to reside in their land permanently.

From the view of the Tasmanian Aboriginal on Van Diemen's Island, earlier visitors who came and went were friendly and cordial. They equally respected each other, except for the sealers, whose industry employed a variety of people, not necessarily English. Social relationships had been at least unthreatening and pleasant. The Tasmanian Aboriginals were later encountered by a foreign "white" people with a mysteriously alien habit of stepping forth upon generally nonwhite people's lands, disregarding the people who inhabited them, whose ancestors had inhabited these lands for thousands of years, planting a stick with some sort of cloth covered with a design, and in the name of some king or nation, thousands of miles away, proclaiming ownership of these lands in the name of their people. From the beginning of their encountering each other, there had been grave misunderstandings.

The foreigners knew humans had been inhabiting the island for a hundred years. They had been unseen by the ships which often stopped on the island to replenish their stock and take on fresh water, but traces and evidence of human residents were taken notice of as early as March 5, 1772, a Frenchman, Captain Marion du Fresne anchored his ships: The

Mascarin and the Marquis de Castries on the west coast of the island, a little south of Tasman's landfall. The small boats landed somewhat to the northwest of what is now, North Bay.

From the beginning, these people experienced a clash in cultural and religious understanding. Quite innocently, the sailors lit a fire, an element sacred to the Aborigine. The lighting of a fire to the Aborigine was only to be done by one so designated among them, a headman, equal to a priest in the other's culture. Fire, being deemed a sacred object to the Aborigine as well as to many other ancient Aboriginal people.

The Aboriginals rained down upon the sailors—a barrage of stones followed by wooden spears, some well aimed, which wounded du Fresne and another officer.

The Frenchmen aboard ship immediately retaliated, firing a fusillade which wounded several and killed one Tasmanian among them, whereupon the rest retreated back into the bush. Succeeding encounters with a variety of Aboriginal were more successful.

Several estimates of Tasmanians at the time of the arrival of the white race, number the Aboriginal from eight thousand to seven hundred, in one location of the island. Other estimates range from seven thousand to two thousand. It is believed that this group on the island might have migrated from the groups on the Australian mainland although the human type and culture were quite different. The Tasmanians were taller and well developed. They had broad wooly heads and a much more wide—nostril broad nose. Early visitors had noted their pleasant disposition, outgoing personality, and fearless demeanor. They were a Nomadic people, having and transporting few possessions. The men were hunters while the women were gatherers of berries and foodstuff. The men had their spears, the tips hardened after sharpening in the fire and a large stick they called, their waddie.

They mainly chose to live as they had always, within the forest and might have conversed among themselves, commenting on the strange white people who had initially come to live on their island, initially not understanding it was to be a permanent arrangement which would threaten and change their lifestyle. Occasionally, in the beginning of the settlements, a band of Aborigine would suddenly emerge from the bush, the women nude, swinging babies from a back sling made of kangaroo skin, the ample-sized privates of the men, swinging along in view as well as the privates of the women exposed. The white missionaries would scurry out with clothing generously donated by Englishmen back home by which to cover their nakedness. Sometimes the material was entirely inappropriate for the hot climate of Australia and its environs. It is said the Aborigine would courteously wear it during their generally short stay in the village and discard them as they returned to the bush. There, they eventually secluded themselves in isolation away from the ever-increasing number of strangers.

Meanwhile, back in England supply ships were often late. Life for the English settlers grew difficult and intolerable for the prisoners who escaped, swelling the numbers of bushrangers. Bushrangers joined up with some of the Aborigine, inciting and encouraging them to join on raids against settlers. Incidents occurred where Aborigines were blamed for acts they did not commit. When Aborigines were caught, whether guilty or innocent, the Aborigines were burned alive over flames, hung, shot, or murdered by other means.

Other bushrangers already psychologically disenfranchised by circumstances in which they found themselves oftentimes legitimately insane, waged continuous attacks upon these once gentle, dark-skinned, and defenseless primitive people.

Bushrangers, sealers, and disreputable stock keepers were guilty of their genocide as well as free settlers, shepherds, and religious ministers. A leading minister the Rev. Thomas Knoppwood, who though kind to the natives during the period before the Aborigine became suspicious and objecting to their circumstance, came to reason that, "the white man, had arrived at receiving these lands due to his having the grace of 'God' so bestowing these lands upon him." A common white Christian concept often heard in many usurped lands, justifying his actions by divine interpretation conceived by whites.

Seldom was punishment meted out to the white man, for the many atrocities against the Aborigine, although reams of documents remain of correspondence between local authorities in the colony and English officials in England, directing justice for these native people. Justice which local authorities were undermanned to carry out if the will of the local authorities had been amenable to ideas of this justice. When the Aboriginal finally went on the offensive in defense of his land, he no longer had the slightest chance of recouping any territory.

Although the initial taking of Tasmania cannot be attributed to racism, the people who encountered and in so many ways killed off the Tasmanian were among the most depraved, degenerated, immoral people of England. Their character was the principle reason England had gone to such lengths to rid herself of them, from their native country. They were the uneducated, as at the time, education was reserved for the privileged. They were the poor white class, bolstered by a warped view of themselves fostered by a mundane religion, the more related to Hinduism than Judaism, originally the religion of the Semitic Hebrew people, which even at this time in history had undergone reinvention or reinterpretation and adjustments by a people, to which it does not historically relate. By 1717, social conditions in England had not improved. Earlier since 1618, white English criminals had been regularly shipped out to North America, the West Indies, and Minorca in Spain's Balearic Province, which periodically fell into English possession during their periodic wars.

Other lamentable English souls were kidnapped by British press gangs, often drugged or bludgeoned senselessly finding themselves aboard ships at sea, as involuntary crew or even sold into slavery. In 1717, a new parliamentary law was passed; everyone charged and convicted of offenses against the Crown were liable to serve seven years transported. These were of accusations of the most petty crimes as begging in areas where they might come into contact with the wealthy classes to accusations leading to convictions of graver crimes.

Those reprieved from the executioner were to serve fourteen years. Contractors for their services to be in the more far removed colonies to acquire a profit from their services. At an earlier time, the Crown had paid five pounds for their outward passage, just to be rid of them.

By 1767, Scottish prisoners of war, anti-Cromwellities, Irish bandits followers of James Scott; Duke of Monmouth, illegitimate son of Lucy Walter, mistress of Charles II, and others were at various times sent into slavery. Voluntary serfs, their alternative, starvation, who sold themselves brought ten pounds a piece for a five-year contract. Prisoners of war fifteen pounds with a more lengthy period of servitude. Blacks were condemned for life and brought fifteen to twenty pounds. The war for independence in the Americas had ended Britain's profitable business with the colonies while the number of prisoners increased at home and English society was unable to cope with her problems.

Simultaneously, the authorities in England concurred with the same thoughts as governor king in Australia. There had to be a territorial expansion of penal properties. Some of the white prisoners had been transported to Africa, but their high death rate made the venture unprofitable.

In England, a lack of prison facilities had caused the officials to house them on ships' hulks in irons. There hulks were overcrowded, unsanitary, verminous, and filthy. Prisoners were laden with body lice. Disease carrying rodents boldly scurried about the chained feet of prisoners and keepers. Men and boys were kept in irons. These included degenerates and lunatics all the more jaded by their condition. Children once recorded as young as age two, more generally from ages twelve to sixteen. Such were the conditions in 1785, when the authorities remembered Captain James Cook's accounts of his explorations to Australia.

By 1802, between six thousand and 7,00G prisoners of all types had been dispatched from England to New South Wales. The crowded insufficient facilities in the homeland were reproduced in the colony. Local officials deemed it essential to create an extension of territory. A flood of communication to effect the expansion was sent to authorities back home. The actual settlement of Van Diemen's Island by the British did not await official instruction from the authorities in England. An indiscreet French captain, visiting at a social gathering in Port Jackson, Australia, revealed his country's intentions to establish a presence on Van Diemen's Island to an English officer. This information was brought to the attention of governor king of the mainland colonies. The French ships and their crew had already sailed on November 18. An English ship was hastily dispatched to overtake the French ships and their crews. The English ship and her crew of seventeen, sighted the two French ships anchored off the east coast of Kings Island. Lt. Charles Robbins, in charge of the English expedition, boarded the French ship, the *Naturaliste* and informed the commander of the Baudin expedition of England's intention to establish their presence at the site.

On December 14, in full sight of the French ships, a contingency of English marines were sent ashore. They hoisted the English colors, in the fashion of Europeans, taking possession of European unclaimed land oblivious to indigenous, native people. A volley of gunpowder was fired, saluting the occasion, and guards were posted at the site. Acknowledging the claim, the French ships departed, sailing for the Gulf of Carpentaria.

The British government, having been informed of the need and intention, agreed to these actions and determined to form a settlement at Port Phillip, on Van Diemen's island. Government officials selected Lt. David Collins as its lieutenant governor. Governor king determined a settlement to be established at the east side of the island at Storm Bay and at Bass Straits on the islands western side. A settlement was established at Port Dalrymple and Lt. John Bowen was sent to establish a settlement on the islands south side, on the Derwent river. By the time Lt. Davy Collins and his party arrived and disembarked ashore, they were met by at least two hundred angry Aborigines. Gone were the earlier pleasant social experiences with people from other nations who had not come to stay. Quite rightly, the Tasmanian were growing suspicious and hostile to the intentions of these white strangers. Extending settlements were a growing concern to all. Collins' men used firearms to disperse the mob. One was killed, three injured. Collins removed from the port, declaring it unsuitable for a colony, and his group reassembled to Port Dalrymple on the north side of the island.

The Tasmanians were besieged by unscrupulous foreigners from the beginning of their meeting with them. This is evidenced by the atrocities of the sealers, who plied their trade of seat skins adjacent to their island, abducting Aboriginal women. From sealers to the British, these ill-fated people were beyond physical atrocities, deprived of their lands and their freedom to pursue their time-honored lifestyle. They were afflicted by the white man's diseases, which he carried to them as he had carried to all aboriginal people throughout the world; respiratory diseases, measles, chicken pox, typhoid, syphilis, gonorrhea, and a number of other venereal diseases. Tasmanian women, abducted by sealers, reportedly killed their half-caste children.

By 1804, the Black War commenced formally, intending to remove their offensive, countenance from the earth. These wars concluded some twenty-six years later in 1830. In 1835, Missionary George Rovinson persuaded the remaining two hundred Tasmanian survivors settled on Flinders Island on the northern coast of Tasmania. Even here, they were cheated by unscrupulous stock keepers. The British government had dispatched seventy head of sheep for each head of family's use and ownership. These were siphoned off by and in their place, salt port and dried beans were substituted.

Wrenched from their beloved island, which the Aborigine often gathered together and watched from afar. Physically restricted from it, massacred, degraded, bewildered by their confrontation with this white scourge of humanity, the Aborigine ceased to propagate. They lost the will to live. Afflicted by alien diseases and malnutrition, within seven years, their numbers dwindled to fifty. The last full-blooded male died in 1869, the last female in 1876.

Although none of their kin were left to tell their side of their story, the effects which came to alight upon their lives, their land and circumstances, we may all envision their plight from the reams of reports, regarding the taking of their land and the state of affairs which came to bear upon them. Accounts official and social of English records and correspondence written by hopeless and helpless inept regional officials and those who would do good hampered by the predicament surrounding them, sometimes to attempt to do good would have threatened their lives, even the lives of their families.

Accounts of the Tasmanian black Aboriginals are herein included, as tales of these and all Asiatic black people are not widely explored and open to the public in the United States other than specific academic institutions and generally white scholars of South Asia as in Midwestern institutions where there are a smaller number of black students as at the Michigan State University. Prior to the advent o f the computer era, I understand it was just as difficult for them to communicate with us, many of whom are now as we are, mainly a racially mixed people. Some of these people made it to England, to the University of London, where there is an Institute of Commonwealth Studies. Others are fine-tuning their communication skills in universities in Australia. Two outstanding brilliant Aborigines have World Wide Web sites: Gary Foley and Mozley.

Mozley can be directly communicated with via the Internet at abc.nett.au/frontier/edu/mozley.htm, and you can communicate with Gary Foley, who is an Australian black activist, actor, adult university student at the University of Melbourne, Australia, by surfing in both at g.foley@ugrad.unimelb.edu.au, and his personal Web site where you may access his brilliant essays on the regional black struggle at http://oliv.com.au/foley.

This publication has been undertaken specifically to address little explored information regarding what I believe is essential information for further exploration by the people earlier known as the American Negro.

I specifically challenge these people to explore the Asiatic black people, as I challenge the white man's theory that the first man arose up on his haunches in Africa, and from there in East Africa reproduced and then migrated out into the wider areas of the globe.

Reason, growing out of the knowledge that the greater number of mankind has for centuries lived in Asia, would tend to back the idea that the single ancestor first singularly arose only in Africa, demands challenging. I propose that at that time, a number of the species arose all over the East Africa-Asia region.

I am not saying that the European white man did not descend from the ancestor, who stood up in East Africa. I am willing to concede that "his" ancestors, the ancestors of the original white man, did indeed migrate up out of those who were in East Africa. I am merely stating that there were others who also stood up in Asia, where all men under any circumstances were and are indigenously dark skinned.

Among the many questions which might arise from the reader is to inquire why bother to compile that of which I have herein related, that which I have been privileged to hear and refer to of readings I have read. I have done so as we are now living in a time of great change. The nation and the whole of the world are changing, and yet we, the American Negro, are yet struggling to find answers to our lost identity. Let there be no mistake; I am not referring to the identity of the myriad of black people who have now immigrated to the United States and who know much of their history, including immigrants from other countries, including those immigrants from the West Indies, all of whom have freely chose to come to these shores.

These people bear a similar resemblance but are not the same people emanating from within Africa, from the same regions.

Under no circumstances should any other group vie to speak for us. They should have the privilege to only speak for themselves. Many people of my kind, the American Negro, respect these people, where respect is due, the same as Korean, Russian, Japanese, Chinese, and Jewish immigrants. Respecting each other's differences and cultures. We expect them to speak for themselves but do not appreciate them when ill-advised; they attempt to speak for us. It is expected that those who read these works will condemn, but it is hoped that before you condemn, you will explore, investigate, and research all of which I have written.

There are areas of common interest. That is of what I have written of the Romans of their having been at ancient times, when they first came to Rome, having been a black people, a nonwhite people from a region of the world with a philosophy of denial of he indigenous self, with a religious understanding of breeding themselves ever lighter and brighter. The fairer skin in reverence to appear as nearly alike as their Aryan conquerors. Then, there is the matter of researching the church, which innocently or not taught the white, European people that the holy families were Nordic, as themselves.

I believe that the scholarly study of the Hindustani people has been deliberately neglected in the West and that study of this dynamic country must be widely explored in the West, by Western scholars who should undertake to give credit to these people of their contributions to Western culture. Also to reveal what great contributions and roles the people of India and her environs played in the actual building and construction of European institutions as well as what we may think of as European philosophy.

I refer to the development of European philosophy as; I believe Hindustani philosophy flowed up westward to ancient Greece along with ancient Egyptian philosophy, which is at least given some credit in the development of Greece. But no credit is given to Hindustan. In Benghazi, in Libya, I once had a colleague who had been studying in Britain and whose visa had expired, and he was forced to leave out of England. He said to me, "We built Europe for them, and now they don't want us there." These words astonished me. He further shared with me his understanding that the Pakistani and Hindustani people had participated in the actual construction of post-Roman, modern European building of great cathedrals and institutions of learning. That his people were the ones who stood on the towering scaffolds and were the bricklayers who had constructed the towering cathedrals, which became the religious fashion of European towns and villages. I believe him. The great builders of the modern world being of Italian extraction today, even in the United States. People invent methods and build upon these ideas and methods; just as when people migrate from one place to another, they carry with them the seeds of what they have known, cherished, and practiced from whence they have come. African people migrated to a region of the world where the environment from which they came in the East had differing environmental resources. On these long arduous journeys, the elders who had knowledge died along the way. The younger and physically stronger had not necessarily had the time to learn of these methods.

The other and an equally great people, who have obviously influenced our being as well as the development of the Western world, have been those people who prefer to be known of as "the Jews." A term, we often unconsciously confuse with the people we call "the Hebrews." I can bear witness personally, that the people who reside on what we in error call "the Middle East," is a great potpourri of people engaging in racial integration. All contributing to what I term *secondary whites*, such as today's Pakistani, Greeks, what I suspect are Bosnians, Albanians, Turkish, Romanians, and Kosovo people. Such people have all migrated to West and run into conflict with earlier settled purer white people and land and space not being finite; they have run into natural disputes and engaged in wars not only for resources but land space. Some among these white Jews have no doubt grown out of integrating racial mixtures with the Semitic Hebrew people. A Semite being a racial mixture of India and Africa. Perhaps such are those among the Cahane who carry the genetic traits of the Lembe who carry the greater number of similar genetic traits.

The larger, however, descend from the Khazar, whose leader, the Grand Khaqan, adopted the Hebrew people's religion during the reign of Solomon the Wise, who ruled in the city-state of Jerusalem in 978 BC. In those days, when the ruler adopted a religion, it was the custom of the populace to follow suit. This occurred in the region of Kazakhstan province, in the South Central region of the former Soviet Union. No doubt, they migrated westward along with the Hindustani people as camp followers.

Like the Roman Hindi, they deigned to become whiter, blue eyed, and blonder as were the original white people. They also encourage these ideas as the standard of beauty and desirability to emulate upon aft the darker races with whom they have come into contact, among people who might differ in opinion who find it the more comfortable to be and accepted as themselves, as they naturally are.

What a man believes, in regarding to the godhead, should be between himself and his concept of God. But make no mistake, the Judeo-Christian expects of you, political allegiance locally as well as loyalty and internationally with the Jewish interests of the contemporary state of Israel. Thus men would be wise to clarify within their minds their concept of the divine, their ideas of creation and that which they deem as the concept of the afterlife in light of contemporary circumstances and all of which I have explored herein and which I hope you will further research and document. I reiterate. In Asia, black people moved racially, in an upward spiral, enjoining in what I must explicitly define as sexual lust and activity for and with the white woman. In Asia, the black man has been the greater precursor of his own genocide.

In great error, we have all too often accused the general white man of such. Heavens knows his crimes of racism against humanity appear numerous, especially those infractions against colored people committed by the British, although I believe that some of the criminals have been of what I term, secondary whites rather than those who descend from original white people. These secondary whites being the character of people who have racially integrated among them. I have earlier identified those whom I believe are the principle character influences among British nonwhite integrators; the early integrated Romans and those people who we term, *the Jewish*. I believe in great error, we have never considered the influence of the personalities of the integrated people impacting upon those with whom they have by sex enjoined. In fact, no study or consideration of the effect or impacting of racial integration has ever been conducted; yet most people in the world are products of one or another type of racial integration. Enjoining with the Chinese in Asia or with the Africans, Asians, and Orientals beyond their regions. It is even implied that some type of Indonesian association has specifically occurred, creating the people we term, *the Japanese*, who are most probably at the pinnacle of the most beautiful people on the globe.

The availability of modern technology in entering into your homes, opening the window of the world should by now have revealed to you the largess of black and colored people yet emerging out of the colored cocoon. And much of such integration has been embraced anciently due to economic, social privileges.

That is to affirm peace treaties growing out of warfare in ancient times. In many of the more primitive societies in Asia, there is yet an unwritten understanding or expectation of wide scale marriages between people of two nations, expecting some sort of mutual allegiance. Even in peace time, generally following battles of war and conquest, large number of white people have been forcibly transported inland as in the case of Georgians into inner Europe, within the proximity of other nonwhite people where they have become accessible to darker tribes with whom they have traded their daughters in marriage for goods by which their greater numbers have sustained themselves.

Go into the stacks of surviving great libraries and "check it out."

Why make an issue of these matters? Because even as we communicate, I accuse those who own, design the more outdated communications controls, of changing ideas within earlier written books to conform with controls regarding what "they" want you to "think" to be plotting as to how they can re-reign your thinking into their approved mind-set. Even the Bible, wherein it was written quoting Solomon, "I am black and comely." It has recently been changed to read in updated versions, "I am brown and comely." And I bet, your mind distorted by the new world order wherein men are hard-pressed to think of much other than the new economy and the high cost of living, you have not had time to reread this and other changes.

English and European history is interesting. However, to you and the entire so-called developing world, I say, it is not your history and we must, beyond the history and interest of the European world, write of our own past experiences, which will require much research from non-Europeanized methods. Myth must be reexamined, uncovered, and plausible facts emerge. We must write of our own, respecting others' differences.

United Nations demographic figures have deemed only 20 percent of the globe's people are white people; these, their figures do not differentiate my difference of primary and secondary whites, meaning 80 percent are nonwhite. A remarkable statement when all over the face of the earth, there are large number of people who being even only slightly fairer than their darker brothers, they refer to themselves as "white," even when they are of the same mother and father. And now in this modern time, representatives of all of these groups have flowed into the United States where they have come and found this is a country wherein you do not come and define yourself but where one is defined.

Representatives of Canadian television defer of buying United States television as it is said, "Their people find little or no interest in United States television fare." In fact, the offerings of the limited people and their lifestyles depicted have declining interest to people here in this country. They do not reflect the lifestyle or interest of the broad mass of people in this country. The broad masses of diverse people with diverse lifestyles in the country are not fooled.

Neither the broad mass of traditional Christian black nor white are in concert with the people who bring us the Jerry Springer television presentation designed to reveal over the airways the very base and lowest moral elements of this society.

The actions of the characters are neither promoted by decent people within this society but are shown worldwide and presented to a world of included colored people as the norm. The semi-literate who allow themselves to be so used for fifteen minutes of fame before the camera are either ignorant or hard-pressed for the shekels they receive for their presence.

The Saviors' Day 2000 convention of the Nation of Islam, in calling for a world of unity of all Muslims was most significant and adherence to such an illustrative clarion will lend great credence to Minister Farakhan as one of the two real black leaders within this country and among those of the nonwhite world.

The other unquestionable leader, one who lays himself on the line in conducting efforts for justice on behalf of blacks is Rev. Al Sharpton, whether you like either one of them or not. A main point is, no black leaders need be again appointed by any other than from among the black diaspora.

Again reiterate, the main purpose I have documented this effort is to inform you of what I believe are some the most significant matters which came to my attention during my unusual journey outside of this country, beyond the constraints and regions of control by forces within this country. People don't realize how much they are being controlled. And the controls are there in order to prescribe and proscribe your mind thereby limiting it. These controls are sometimes conducted by the forces of organized religion which even go about within the old world, in order to dilute and subjugate communication of people who know their own history.

More and more is forthcoming today, out of the third world. You have been permitted to hear of the black Jews of Ethiopia who were brought out of Uganda and now you have been permitted to hear of the Lombe of South Africa, of whom it has been revealed, carry the same genetic code as the Cohene of Israel, possibly of whom are products with these people anciently by racial integration; a subject of which the "white" Jews know much and have practiced worldwide.

Again I reiterate; It is hoped that you, the young, take these few ideas I have shared with you herein and research them and conduct further explorations into the implications of these ideas. Again, I repeat, I believe the most important of these have been the fact that I affirmed in England, that the ancient Romans, who migrated originally to the seven hills, came from India.

I state, on the basis of Roman historic research, that they transported their most highly racially integrated dissidents to the British Isles and that other now, highly racially integrated citizens fled Rome to the British Isles with their enormous portable wealth as the empire fell into decline.

Most import, the princes of the land became the princes of the Holy Roman Catholic Church, the new world order for continuing Roman rule. The more things changed, the more they remained the same. Most significant for us, the church, affirmed Racism, a credo of the church, not so much as a verbal statement but by having artists depicting the dark-skinned holy Semitic families depicted as Nordics. The Holy Roman Catholic Church was not initially created to entice nonwhites and such as the horde of faithful Asiatics who ascribe to the faith today. In time, however, their adherence to Catholicism delivered large amounts of gold, property, and other amenities which embellished the coffers of the organization now enriched and its influence widespread. This universal entity was designed for Northwestern European whites. These intended worshipers were created in the imagery as depicted on the walls, windows, and edifices of the European church. The message, to be taken as infallible.

Although many are suspicious that the whole of the white world is racist, there is another side of the coin, a new one to be considered. Seeing ourselves, as other people see us, especially the new black immigrants.

One worth mentioning is Attorney Dr. Khlid Abdullah Tariq Al-Mansour. He is from an undescribed African country, which may include Arabia Felix, which he appropriately describes as Northeast Africa, the manner by which Arabia is described by African-Arabs. Certainly, I can personally affirm there is little or no difference between indigenous Arabs in Arabia and many Africans in Africa.

Dr. Al-Mansour, in one of his timely essays on his published Web site World-hi.com, take issue with the African American family organization, the Thomas Woodson Family Association. They are the descendants of Sally Hemmings and Thomas Jefferson. Dr. Al-Mansour, like many other people of and in Africa, appear perplexed by black Americans, who ascribe to pride in associating themselves as pleased by white blood from known American racist.

He also takes aim at the NAACP, without exclamation and charges it as having the unique ability to pursue the absurd. It would be wise, therefore, to screen out people, who come and sit among us as if they were a part and parcel of our unique community. Earlier black immigrants, who came, certainly enjoined, for any opportunities they might find here, unavailable in lands and islands from which they had come.

The new world order, however, has enlarged the community here on the mainland as well as globally. We must enlarge the scope of our thinking to embrace it as well as become an active part of it.

At long last, recognition will be given to blacks in Australia, opening up the way for all blacks in the outer lands easterly to participate in the global black community. Even an assessment of the singleness of human ancestry must be rethought. It is highly possible that the ancestry of Germanics, Finns, Vikings, and other Northwestern European white tribes came up out of East Africa's region. But did all of the initial whites emanate from India?

Every black professional must now write something regarding what he has to say to descending black posterity. Preferably on his opinions, perhaps regarding his field of expertise. Sociologists need to write, and if they own a computer and printer, publish their own works. A source of bookbinding machines is identified at the end of this volume.

# REFERENCES

Clive Turnbull, (1965) *Black War*, Cheshire-Lansdowne, Melbourne

Prof. James P. Campbell, *Oriental Mythology*, HarperCollins Publishers

Will Durant, (1954) *Our Oriental Heritage*, Simon & Shuster,

L. W. King, *History of Babylon*

Prof. Philip K. Hitti, *History of the Arabs*, St. Martin's Press, New York City

*A History of the Jews in Christian Spain*, The Jewish Publication Society of America in Philadelphia

Grateful acknowledgment to the head of the Institute of Commonwealth Studies, University of London, Russel Square, London; librarian, University of London, School of Oriental and African Studies; people in and of Indonesia, Bangladesh, Sri Lanka, South India, and northern Nigeria to whom I am grateful and most honored to have had them share with me their knowledge.

www.ingramcontent.com/pod-product-compliance
Lightning Source LLC
Chambersburg PA
CBHW071032080526
44587CB00015B/2577